A Teacher's Introduction to Deconstruction

A Teacher's Introduction to Deconstruction

Sharon Crowley
Northern Arizona University

NCTE Teacher's
Introduction Series

National Council of Teachers of English
1111 Kenyon Road, Urbana, Illinois 61801

I dedicate this book to the memory of my parents, teachers both: Dorothy Parriott Conway and J. A. Conway.

NCTE Editorial Board: Donald R. Gallo, Richard Lloyd-Jones, Raymond J. Rodrigues, Dorothy S. Strickland, Brooke Workman, Charles Suhor, *ex officio*, Michael Spooner, *ex officio*

Staff Editor: Robert A. Heister

Cover Design: Michael J. Getz

Interior Design: Tom Kovacs for TGK Design

NCTE Stock Number 50144–3020

Library of Congress Cataloging-in-Publication Data

Crowley, Sharon, 1943-
  A teacher's introduction to deconstruction / Sharon Crowley.
    p.   cm. — (NCTE teacher's introduction series)
  Bibliography: p.
  ISBN 0–8141–5014–4
  1. English language—Rhetoric—Study and teaching.
  2. Deconstruction. I. Title.
  PE1404.C76 1989
  808'.042'07—dc19
                                                                89-2887
                                                                CIP

Contents

Foreword

With the publication of *A Teacher's Introduction to Deconstruction*, we begin what we hope will be a new series of books that are especially useful to teachers of English and language arts at all levels. Ours is a wide-ranging discipline, and important scholarly developments in various aspects of our field can be highly complex, not to mention voluminous. We often wish we had the time to take courses or do extended personal reading in topics such as deconstruction, psycholinguistics, rhetorical theory, and the like. Realistically, each of us can read intensively and extensively only in those areas that are of special interest to us or that are most closely related to our work. The Teacher's Introduction Series, then, is geared towards the intellectually curious teacher who would like to get an initial, lucid glance into rich areas of scholarship in our discipline.

Let me stress three things that are *not* intended in *A Teacher's Introduction to Deconstruction* and in future books that will appear in this series. First, the books are in no way shortcuts to in-depth knowledge of any field. Rather, these straightforward treatments are intended to provide introductions to major ideas in the field and to whet the appetite for further reading. Hence, bibliographies and suggestions for further reading are included. Second, the books do not aim to "dumb down" complicated ideas, sanitizing them for an imagined "average reader." Many of the ideas are quite challenging, and we don't seek to patronize the reader by watering them down. Third, we don't want to send the message that every subject which is important to English and language arts teachers should be taught directly in the classroom. The personal enrichment of the teacher is paramount here. An understanding of the complexities of deconstruction might or might not come to inform Monday morning activities; but our primary goal is to provide stimulating texts for English teachers at all levels and not necessarily to provide specific classroom applications. A great deal of misery might have been avoided in the 1960s if teachers had been doubly urged to learn about grammars new and old—that's part of being a well-rounded teacher—but to *avoid* bringing their new insights, tree diagrams and all, directly into the classroom.

We are grateful to Sharon Crowley for taking on the formidable work of writing the first book in the Teacher's Introduction Series, especially since deconstruction is a topic that doesn't strike graceful poses for explicators (perhaps appropriately, as Crowley points out). In discussing development of the text with the author, I wrote "Knowing your subject in its complexity, you'll need to play Coleridge and 'bring the wonders down' without doing violence to the ideas as you simplify them. This isn't quite the compositional equivalent of walking on water, but it does involve some fancy footwork, and I think you're up to it." As you read *A Teacher's Introduction to Deconstruction*, I think you'll agree that Dr. Crowley was indeed up to the task.

Charles Suhor
Deputy Executive Director
NCTE

Introduction

One of the many paradoxes in the history of English departments has been the unacknowledged—even unperceived—influence of literary theory on the undergraduate and secondary teaching of English. It is not difficult, for instance, to trace the assumptions of New Criticism from their sources (for instance, Wellek's and Warren's *Theory of Literature* and Brooks's *The Well Wrought Urn*) through literature classes and into composition, as do James Berlin in *Rhetoric and Reality: Writing Instruction in American Colleges, 1900–1985* (1987, 107–111) and, more extensively, Colleen Aycock in her 1984 dissertation "New Critical Rhetoric and Composition."

Every English teacher acts on the basis of theory. Unless teaching is a random series of lessons, drills, and readings, chosen willy-nilly, the English class is guided by theories of language, literature, and pedagogy. That is, insofar as teachers choose readings and plan instruction, they are *implementing* a theory. The question, of course, is whether or not teachers understand the theory that guides their instruction. If we do not understand the theoretical context in which we function, we are powerless—unable to rationalize what we do and hence stripped of the ability to argue our case with administrators, boards of education, governments, and special interest groups such as, for example, those advocating or condemning bilingual education.

The current theoretical era in literary studies and composition/rhetoric can fairly be called post-structuralist, the methods and assumptions of structuralism having run their course, superseded now by other schools, notably reader-response criticism and deconstruction, the latter a particularly radical and furiously complex body of doctrine that has been extraordinarily influential in both literary studies and composition/rhetoric.

I would like to stipulate that Romanticism and the New Criticism set the stage for the reception of deconstruction, the subject of Sharon Crowley's admirable and admirably concise guide for teachers. Whether or not my historical argument will stand up is beside the point of this introduction. What does matter is the guidance through an excruciatingly difficult body of theory that Professor Crowley provides.

In bare essence, the project of deconstruction is to obliterate the doctrine of presence in Western metaphysics—that is, to deconstruct the all-pervasive notion that behind the words is *a* truth that the words express. (And if there were, how could that truth be expressed, except in words?) Deconstruction, then, razes determinate meaning and from the rubble constructs the indeterminate text, behind which or within which there is no single, unvarying meaning.

If one dates the beginning of deconstruction in English departments from the publication of Gayatri Chakravorty Spivak's translation of Derrida's *Of Grammatology* in 1976, that movement has been around for some thirteen years now, and its impact can be seen in, for example, Hillis Miller's "Composition and Decomposition: Deconstruction and the Teaching of Writing" (1983); *Writing and Reading Differently: Deconstruction and the Teaching of Composition and Literature* (1985), edited by G. Douglas Atkins and Michael Johnson; and the witty, iconoclastic *Plato, Derrida, Writing* (1988), by Jasper Neel.

As Crowley's bibliography demonstrates, the profession has responded to deconstructionist theory in typical fashion, with a plethora of *supplements,* every text being an occasion for further textuality, *ad infinitum.* The sources of this weighty lode—for example, *Of Grammatology*—are daunting in the specialized knowledge one needs to understand them and in the barrier created by the coy rhetoric of authors such as Derrida and his epigones. Most of us would be grateful for assistance in getting the gist of a philosophical position that for at least a decade has been central to discussions of literature and that, by laws as inexorable as those of plate tectonics, will influence the teaching of English for decades to come. Crowley's explanation of deconstruction, in her first chapter, is reliable, balanced, and accessible to readers with little background in the underlying epistemological and linguistic issues.

After explaining the basic concepts of deconstruction in her first chapter, Crowley develops an unexceptionable thesis in her second: that prevailing literary theories powerfully influence English department teaching in both literature and composition, and that

> Despite official announcements of their demise, deconstruction and post-structuralism have affected the politics of American departments of English in fundamental ways. In many colleges and universities, literary theory has become a more respectable teaching interest than it once was, and university teachers can now be hired because they are "theorists" or "post-structuralists" rather than "Miltonists" or "Chaucerians." And . . . the new emphasis on literary theory is congenial, in many respects, with the growth of interest in rhetoric and composition theory, fields whose

assumptions about language are sometimes compatible with those
made in post-structuralist thought.

The argument that has obviously been Crowley's real interest all
along is the substance of her third and final chapter: the implications
of deconstructionist theory for composition, namely, the problemati-
zation of traditional doctrines: authorial sovereignty and authority,
"the view that the writing process begins and ends with an individual
author"; "our easy separation of thought from language, content from
form, meaning from expression"; and the distinctions of genre that
have often structured composition courses and textbooks.

It is defensible (though hardly neat and incisive) to say that
composition theories and practices can be classed as text-centered,
author-centered, or transactional. The images are clear: that of pages
in an open book; that of a lone writer producing text; and that of a
writer on one side, a text in the middle, and a reader on the other
side. Crowley sets out to explain how deconstruction might contribute
to a necessary move from the "process" model to the "transactional."

A bit of history will help clarify both Crowley's argument and my
comments on it. In 1891 Harvard tightened up its admission standards
to exclude students who were deficient in writing ability, and in 1897,
the university reduced "general education" requirements to one course:
a year of freshman rhetoric. (Berlin 1984, 58–76 tells the whole story.)
In beefing up standards, Harvard institutionalized current-traditional,
text-centered rhetoric, for the focus was on the mechanical correctness
and even the handwriting of essays completed by applicants for
admission. (Notice that Harvard validated composition as a university
course; therefore, Arkansas and California and South Dakota and Utah
had license to follow suit. Freshman composition became the universal
hurdle for students, the bane of literature faculties, and the life raft
for graduate programs in English.)

A whole synapse or syndrome of stirrings and forces brought about
the shift of focus to the author. Several rebels against current-tradi-
tionalism published lively, iconoclastic, and commercially successful
texts: Macrorie, *Telling Writing;* Elbow, *Writing without Teachers;* Coles,
Composing: Writing as a Self-Creating Process. Research into the composing process began. In 1971, Janet Emig published her seminal
monograph *The Composing Process of Twelfth Graders.* By 1977, Flower
and Hayes were under way with their studies of composing, and in
that year Oxford published Shaughnessy's *Errors and Expectations.* The
point is this: the composing process became an object of scholarly
inquiry. But perhaps most important, the Anglo-American Conference
(Dartmouth Conference) was held in 1966 and reported on in several

volumes, the most influential of which is John Dixon's *Growth through English* (1967), a little book that had enormous impact. At Dartmouth, the Americans were advancing the "heritage" model (that is, the Anglo-American canon of literature) and the "skills" model (for example, grammar exercises). The British, however, won the day with their "growth" model. Now, it is the case that the growth model was salubrious; it moved some teachers away from mere "skills" and opened up the canon—away from the red pencil and veneration of *Adam Bede*—but it had within it a large component of solipsism: the child using language to grow cognitively and emotionally and to discover the world. The image is that of a student communing with himself or herself. At the very least, we can say that the growth model did not emphasize transaction. Yet rhetoricians old and new share a transactional view of "writing" in the broadest sense of that word. The greatest of the old rhetoricians said that rhetoric is the art of finding the available means of persuasion in regard to any subject whatever, and Kenneth Burke, the greatest of the new rhetoricians, says, "You persuade a man only insofar as you can talk his language by speech, gesture, tonality, order, image, attitude, idea, *identifying your ways with his*" (1969, 55).

"Deconstruction," Crowley says, "assumes the complicity of writers and readers in all acts of composing. That is, readers of any discourse become its writers as they reconstruct a 'meaning' for it. . . . A deconstructive pedagogy . . . would redirect the notion of intention or purpose away from examination of a text onto its suitability to the rhetorical situation for which it was designed." Compositionists who consider themselves New Rhetoricians must at this point be heartened. Their allies are a formidable trio—Aristotle, Kenneth Burke, and Jacques Derrida—who, while differing in important respects, support the transactional model.

However, when we consider the tradition in which we English teachers function, the future does not look so bright for those of us who consider ourselves New Rhetoricians and hence transactionalists, for we understand that deconstruction could as easily serve as the foundation for a revival or perpetuation of author-centeredness in composition. Almost offhandedly in chapter two, Crowley remarks, "Of course, a deconstructive pedagogy would locate invention within the movement of language itself, rather than in the individual writer, as much current composition theory does." But locating *invention* in the movement of language itself in effect does away with, or easily can do away with, context (or "scene," as Kenneth Burke would say) and audience. As cases in point, here are, first, Jacques Derrida, followed by Peter Elbow (the most inexorably author-centered of all well-known compositionists):

> It is because writing is *inaugural*, in the fresh sense of the word, that it is dangerous and anguishing. It does not know where it is going, no knowledge can keep it from the essential precipitation toward meaning that it constitutes and that is, primarily, its future. (Derrida 1978, 18)

> . . . think of writing as an organic, developmental process in which you start writing at the very beginning—before you know your meaning at all—and encourage your words gradually to change and evolve. (Elbow 1973, 15)

As I conclude this introduction, I must confess that my reserved tone has been a façade. The "Crowley" of whom I have spoken is, actually, my good friend Sharon, many of whose most important philosophical, scholarly, and personal values are mine also. I know that Sharon belongs to what I have been calling the New Rhetoric and that she is, therefore, a transactionalist. I know also that she is skeptical about the possibility of changing those institutions within which we English teachers must function: schools, colleges, universities; a powerful, text-bound literary establishment; a tradition in which composition is devalued. And I think that is why a tone of melancholy pervades the last words in this admirable book: "Perhaps the best to be hoped for is that a deconstructive critique demonstrates the necessity of continued interrogation of the strategies used to teach reading and writing. I can only hope that this essay has stimulated a few of its readers to engage in such a critique."

W. Ross Winterowd
University of Southern California

References

Atkins, G. Douglas, and Michael L. Johnson, eds. *Writing and Reading Differently: Deconstruction and the Teaching of Composition and Literature.* Lawrence: University Press of Kansas, 1985.

Aycock, Colleen. "New Critical Rhetoric and Composition." Dissertation. University of Southern California, 1984.

Berlin, James A. *Writing Instruction in Nineteenth-Century American Colleges and Universities.* Carbondale: Southern Illinois University Press, 1984.

———. *Rhetoric and Reality: Writing Instruction in American Colleges, 1900–1985.* Carbondale: Southern Illinois University Press, 1987.

Brooks, Cleanth. *The Well Wrought Urn.* New York: Reynall and Hitchcock, 1947.

Burke, Kenneth. *A Rhetoric of Motives.* Berkeley and Los Angeles: University of California Press, 1969.

Coles, William E. *Composing: Writing as a Self-Creating Process.* Rochelle Park, N.J.: Hayden, 1974.

Derrida, Jacques. "Force and Signification." *Writing and Difference.* Translated by Alan Bass. Chicago: University of Chicago Press, 1978: 3–30.

Dixon, John. *Growth through English.* New York: Oxford University Press for the National Association for the Teaching of English, 1967.

Elbow, Peter. *Writing without Teachers.* New York: Oxford University Press, 1973.

Emig, Janet. *The Composing Processes of Twelfth Graders.* NCTE Research Report No. 13. Urbana, Ill.: NCTE, 1971.

Flower, Linda [S]. "Writer-Based Prose: A Cognitive Basis for Solving Problems in Writing." *College English* 41 (1979): 19–37.

————, and John R. Hayes. *A Process Model of Composing.* Document Design Project Technical Report No. 1. Pittsburgh: Carnegie-Mellon University Press, 1979.

Macrorie, Ken. *Telling Writing.* Rochelle Park, N.J.: Hayden, 1970.

Neel, Jasper. *Plato, Derrida, Writing.* Carbondale: Southern Illinois University Press, 1988.

Shaughnessy, Mina. *Errors and Expectations: A Guide for the Teacher of Basic Writing.* New York: Oxford University Press, 1977.

Wellek, René, and Austin Warren. *Theory of Literature.* 3rd ed. New York: Harcourt, 1956.

Preface

When the editors of this series asked me to write the essay that follows, they already had a title in mind for it—it would be called "A Teacher's Introduction to Deconstruction." The piece was to be part of a series of essays that would introduce teachers of English to new developments in rhetorical and literary theory.

I must admit that I had some initial doubts about this project. I worried that its title would imply, somehow, that English teachers required some sort of mediation—a gloss, an interpretation—that could stand between them and the primary texts in which deconstructive strategies are demonstrated and discussed. I also worried that the editors wanted something like "Deconstruction Made Simple," a project which would respect neither the complexity of the subject nor the sophistication of its intended audience.

I finally decided, however, that the mandated title ought to mean something like this: "This essay will help English teachers to see what it is that deconstruction has to offer them as they pursue their work." Deconstruction is, among other things, a theory of reading and writing. And a writing teacher's work is theoretical, after all; a teacher's assumptions about how language works and how best to teach its workings guide every choice she makes, from the books she asks her students to read to the exercises she asks them to complete. This observation holds whether these assumptions are implicit or explicit in her teaching. I hope that the essay which follows will demonstrate the advantages for teaching of making any theory of reading and writing explicit.

As I wrote this essay, then, I tried to focus on the implications of deconstruction for the English classroom in American schools. What happened as I wrote was not entirely what I expected. While I was following up the implications of deconstruction for English teaching, I found that I was also performing a deconstructive reading of some traditional English pedagogies of reading and writing. This happened (I think) because deconstructive notions call into question many of the assumptions that are often made about the processes of native-language reading and writing, and about how these processes are learned and taught. As a result of this work, then, I found myself deconstructing what might be called the academic ideology that governs a good deal of literacy instruction in American schools.

Since it is limited to unraveling the ramifications of deconstruction for English teaching, there are a couple of things that this essay does not do. First of all, its account of deconstruction focuses on those aspects of deconstructive thought that have serious potential for altering our thinking about reading and writing pedagogies. As a consequence, it ignores hefty portions of the primary texts in which deconstruction was introduced to American readers, especially those having to do with the history of philosophy. Deconstruction is a fairly esoteric strategy of reading, developed by a French philosophy teacher named Jacques Derrida so that he could undertake a wide-ranging critique of Western philosophy. Derrida thinks that traditional philosophy binds and distorts our thinking about the relations between self-consciousness, thought, and language. Traditional thought about these matters promotes a number of powerful and yet unspoken assumptions that have blinded Westerners to the deceptive nature of speech and writing and their role in human activities. The project called "deconstruction" attempts to expose these assumptions for what they are.

Consequently, Derrida has concentrated much of his attention on re-reading the major texts of Western philosophy, in an attempt to expose the workings in them of what he calls "the metaphysics of presence." However, because his initial interests lay with the deconstruction of a strictly philosophical tradition, Derrida's readings of the work of figures like Edmund Husserl, Immanuel Kant, and Sigmund Freud are relevant to this essay only indirectly.

Second, although it provides an overview of some of Derrida's thought, this essay is emphatically not an introduction to, or outline of, the work of Jacques Derrida—as though one could write a sort of "Cliffs Notes" on Derrida and deconstruction. There are several excellent books in print that are intended to introduce Derrida's work to American readers. The most accessible of them are, in order, Jonathan Culler's *On Deconstruction* (1982); Christopher Norris's *Deconstruction: Theory and Practice* (1982); and Vincent Leitch's *Deconstructive Criticism: An Advanced Introduction* (1983). But anybody who reads this essay, or Culler's, or anyone else's, in the hope of skipping the work of reading Derrida's texts will be cheated. Any summary of, or commentary on, Derrida's texts is necessarily reductive, or "supplementary," as Derrida might say. Derrida's writing is notoriously difficult (there are good reasons for this, as I hope to establish). But it always repays the close attention it demands from readers. Reading Derrida is a lot like reading *Ulysses* or *Finnegans Wake;* it's tough at first, but once you get the hang of it, you find it worth the effort. I hope, then, that readers of this essay who have not yet acquainted themselves with Derrida's work will want to do so. (An appendix to this essay suggests some hints that may help readers who wish to begin reading Derrida.)

Third, although reading and writing are not so easily separated from one another in deconstructive thought as they are in the structure of English departments, I have concentrated on writing instruction in this essay. Aside from a few remarks about traditional literary pedagogy in chapter one, and about the practice of deconstructive criticism in chapter two, I say relatively little about the practice of teaching literature, a lack for which I apologize. Since I am not a teacher of literature, I felt it would be inappropriate for me to make suggestions about how literary pedagogy might incorporate deconstructive insights. However, teachers of literature should not find it difficult to extrapolate Derrida's thought for their own work. Further, the work of the "Yale critics"—Paul de Man, Geoffrey Hartman, and J. Hillis Miller—provides excellent models of deconstructive readings. Teachers of literature can also resort to Gregory Ulmer's *Applied Grammatology* (1985) for an account of a "post(e)-pedagogy" that takes Derrida's thought very seriously. Two textbooks also utilize recent developments in literary theory: Robert Scholes's, Nancy Comley's, and Gregory Ulmer's *Text Book* (1988); and Kathleen McCormick's, Gary Waller's, and Linda Flower's *Reading Texts: Reading, Responding, Writing* (1987).

Fourth, I am aware that on occasion my exposition of Derrida's thought is difficult to read. Most of the difficulty, I hope, can be assigned to the difficulty of the matters he is tackling, and not to my own stylistic insufficiencies. However, I did adopt or adapt some of Derrida's eccentric syntactic mannerisms, such as inversion or fragmentation, when I thought that these underscored or enhanced a point. I apologize in advance to readers who are irritated by any of my departures from convention.

A note about audience: I have assumed throughout this essay that my readers are professional English teachers who know little or nothing about Derrida and deconstruction. However, I also assumed that this essay might attract a few informed readers, who can (and no doubt will) raise objections to what I've said in the text. Many of the endnotes are the result of an imaginary dialogue I carried on with these readers while I wrote.

All works cited are listed in the bibliography, and are cited in the text by date and page number (for example, "1985, 323"). I have made two exceptions to this rule: Derrida's texts are cited by an abbreviated title and page number (for example, "*WD*, 124", which means "*Writing and Difference*, page 124"); and classical texts are cited by standard manuscript line number (for example, "265e"). The bibliography also lists some selected works about deconstruction as well as a few exemplary works of deconstructive criticism.

As Derrida would have it, all the persons named in the next sentences helped to write this essay. They were its readers, or they offered stimulation, support, or counseling to its author. Special thanks to Tilly Warnock, for whom teaching, theorizing, and friendship are commensurable practices. For their responses to, or arguments about, the matters discussed here I thank Gary Eddy, Amy Gingrich, Victor Vitanza, and my students in English 621. Ross Winterowd's disagreement with me about the worth of post-structuralist thought has not kept him from being a friend, advisor, and teller of instructive stories about the English profession. Thanks to Michael Spooner, who talked me into this. A portion of this manuscript will appear in *PRE-TEXT,* vol. 8, no. 3–4. Last of all, I thank Bryan Short, without whom.

Sharon Crowley
Northern Arizona University

1 Reading/Writing Derrida

Jacques Derrida teaches philosophy at the École Normale Supérieure in Paris. His written works which concern us here were published between 1967 and 1972, for the most part. They include two books, *Of Grammatology* (1967) and *Dissemination* (1972); two collections of essays, *Writing and Difference* (1967), and *Margins of Philosophy* (1972); as well as a collection of interviews, *Positions* (1972).

In the "presentation" or introduction to his thesis defence in 1980, Derrida offered a brief history of the work he had carried out during the 1960s, and which resulted in this collection of writings. During this period, he said, he had

> tried to work out ... what was in no way meant to be a system but rather a sort of strategic device, opening onto its own abyss, an unclosed, unenclosable, not wholly formalizable ensemble of rules for reading, interpretation and writing." (Montefiore 1983, 40)

This "strategic device," this set of rules for reading, would be called "deconstruction."

The Metaphysics of Presence

Using this way of reading, Derrida detected a set of themes in the history of philosophy and the human sciences that systematically privileged the human speaking voice, and just as systematically devalued writing. As he put it, he detected

> an evaluation of writing, or, to tell the truth, rather a devaluation of writing whose insistent, repetitive, even obscurely compulsive, character was the sign of a whole set of long-standing constraints. These constraints were practised at the price of contradictions, of denials, of dogmatic decrees ... I proposed to analyse the non-closed and fissured system of these constraints under the name of logocentrism in the form that it takes in Western philosophy and under that of phonocentrism as it appears in the widest scope of its dominion. (Montefiore 1983, 40)

Logos is a word from classical Greek that has meant, variously, "voice," "speech," "law," and, somewhat later, "reason." "Logocentrism" and

1

"phonocentrism" are Derrida's nicknames for the foundational Western philosophical assumption that conscious, integrated selves—spirits, psyches, minds, subjects—are at the center of all human activity. This assumption is "logocentric" because this "self" is tied to words; it is "phonocentric," because the self is manifested in, or represented by, the sounds made by a speaking voice.

Derrida names the set of constraints that permits this assumption to function in Western philosophy "the metaphysics of presence." *Of Grammatology,* a very important work for understanding Derrida's notions about writing, traces an early articulation of the metaphysics of presence to Aristotle. This is not to say that Aristotle "originated" the notions I'm about to describe; the origins of all such complex and fundamental intellectual structures are probably undiscoverable. But because we have access to certain texts that scholarly tradition ascribes to someone named "Aristotle," and because the metaphysics of presence is inscribed, or described, in these texts, Aristotle's name provides a handy umbrella under which we can discuss this complex set of notions.

As an eloquent spokesperson for the metaphysics of presence, Aristotle conceived of language as both a representation of truth and as an instrument for finding it. Language, whether spoken or written, could serve these functions because it represents what all human beings share in common: mind. Derrida quotes a passage from Aristotle's *On Interpretation:*

> Just as all men have not the same writing so all men have not the same speech sounds, but mental experiences, of which these are the *primary symbols (seméia prôtos),* are the same for all, as also are those things of which our experiences are the images. (Book I, 16a; *OG*, 11. Derrida's emphasis.)

Presumably, Aristotle generated this representational attitude toward language simply because he, like all humans, possessed an "inner voice"—that voice (or consciousness, or memory) which assures each of us of our self-identity, indeed, of our "self-present-ness." From this assumption of self-presence, it was an easy step to infer a similar presence, or being-here, of all that seems to exist in the world.

In the *Grammatology,* Derrida explains how the leap from voice to self-presence to Being must have been made:

> The voice, producer of *the first symbols,* has a relationship of essential and immediate proximity with the mind. Producer of the first signifier, it is not just a simple signifier among others. It signifies "mental experiences" which themselves reflect or mirror things by natural resemblance. (11)

That is, our voices (both inner and outer), as well as their continuity throughout our lives, assure us that we do, indeed, exist as a conscious entity having both a present and a past. And by a kind of doubling movement, the relation of signification that exists between voice and mind is transferred to the relation of minds to nature. In other words, the metaphysics of presence assumes two sets of similar relations: as minds represent or signify the substances of nature, so does language represent or signify the "stuff" of minds, and through this, nature. I quote Derrida again:

> Between being and mind, things and feelings, there would be a relation of translation or natural signification; between mind and logos, a relation of conventional symbolization. (*OG*, 11)

Thus traditional metaphysics constructed a self-sealing argument regarding the representative relationships that exist between minds, the world, and language.

Put in its simplest terms, the self-sealing argument goes something like this: minds correctly perceive and experience the world because they have a natural representative relation to it. Further, minds create language, which must perforce represent nature, as well as the workings of minds, since language is a mental production, and thus a product of nature. The word "represent," as I use it here, should be read as a pun: minds not only represent nature in the sense of signifying or symbolizing it; they also quite literally "re-present" it—make it present to us, give it to us again, perfect and undistorted. Minds "picture" nature, if you will.

Aristotle's contemporaries built a grammar based on this double relation between nature and minds, minds and language; Aristotle himself erected a logic from them. In Greek, as in most other Western languages, the simple sentence consists of two terms: a subject—a something or somebody—and a predicate, most often predicating of the subject that it is, that it exists. Assuming that this fundamental grammatical structure somehow represents reality, the next step is to derive a logic from it. Aristotelean logic is based on two concepts borrowed directly from the grammar of the simple sentence—categories and predicables, classes of things and the possible relations between things. The basic assumption of this logic—the law of identity and contradiction—posits that either a thing is or it is not. Of course this law presumed presence, and the entire logical system awarded privilege to identity, rather than to contradiction. Thus, classical grammar and logic conspired with metaphysics to create a neatly closed circle: reality is enshrined in the structure of the language—it is represented in

"subjects" and "categories" that we manipulate by means of "predi-
cates"—and language, especially when systematized into a logic,
becomes an instrument for re-presenting the world and the workings
of mind upon it.

Inscription and Signification

But Derrida wants to point out that both of these assumptions were
made possible, feasible, only because of the inner voice which speaks;
or better, because of the language that gives voice to voices. Derrida
might argue that traditional metaphysical thought about minds, world,
and language has it precisely backwards, or upside down, or inside
out. Consciousness does not precede, and give birth to, language;
rather, it is language that makes consciousness possible. From where
Derrida sits, it might be that signs themselves (or the process of
signifying) preceded minds, rather than the other way around.

But this trade-off, which rejects consciousness as the primary designation of human being, and puts the ability to signify in its place,
is not an entirely happy one. "From this perspective," as Robert Scholes
remarks, "human beings became human by receiving the gift of signs—
at the cost of perceiving nothing but signs, everywhere" (1988, 291).
If this is the case, language itself, which is an infinite series of signs,
dictates that knowing and thinking are processes that are indistin-
guishably bound up with the movement of language. To write a bit
more poetically, language speaks us. Texts are everywhere. As J. Hillis
Miller puts it, perhaps a little recklessly, "language is not an instrument
or tool in man's hands, a submissive means of thinking. Language
rather thinks man and his 'world,' including poems, if he will allow
them to do so" (1977, 444).

Derrida has a term for language, when it is thought about in this
larger, compelling sense: he calls it "arche-writing." Arche-writing
names

> all that gives rise to an inscription in general, whether it is literal
> or not and even if what it distributes in space is alien to the order
> of the voice: cinematography, choreography, of course, but also
> pictorial, musical, sculptural "writing." (*OG*, 9)

Arche-writing is human in-scription on the world's surface, human
re-marking of the landscape. And this inscription, this remarking, is
thoroughly linguistic.

Derrida chooses "writing" to name this nearly unthinkable notion
partly because, in the metaphysics of presence, writing (in its more

literal sense) has always been devalued, secondarized. In the *Grammatology*, he continues his account of the founding gesture of metaphysics by recounting how this devaluation occurred:

> The feelings of the mind, expressing things naturally, constitute a sort of universal language which can then efface itself. . . . All signifiers, and first and foremost the written signifier, are derivative with regard to what would wed the voice indissolubly to the mind or to the thought of the signified sense, indeed to the thing itself. . . . the written signifier is always technical and representative. It has no constitutive meaning. (*OG*, 11)

In order for the metaphysics of presence to get off the ground, its inaugural move—the identification of voice with mind—had to be forgotten; mind had to be privileged over language as the initiating force of human consciousness. That is, mind was regarded as the prime mover of human-ness, while language was demoted to a secondary medium which could only re-present or mimic the movements of mind. The metaphysics of presence chose to forget that the ability to signify—the ability which allowed the privileging of mind in the first place—was precisely the province or function of language.

The mimetic function of language, its transparency, had to be assumed in the metaphysics of presence; as Derrida puts it elsewhere in the *Grammatology*: a "lived reduction of the opacity of the signifier" is "the origin of what is called presence" (166). In other words, in order to retain the myth of the primacy of mind, metaphysics has to look through language, not at it. It has to assume that language is transparent, rather than opaque. Further, it must assume that language has no originary or creative powers of its own. On this model language, especially written language, cannot generate or constitute meaning on its own; it is only instrumental, forever dependent on some other generative force for its motivation.

Thus a double-sided move constituted the fundamental power play of Western metaphysics. The signified (presence, consciousness, self, mind, reality, truth, reason) was elevated over the signifier (language or any other sign system), which was reduced to a pliant medium of representation. Once this move was made, thought became fundamental, primary, and language became derivative—representing, mirroring, or recreating thought. Likewise, metaphysics could become the "first science"—first in both senses, primary and fundamental—because it could ferret out essences which were uncontaminated by language.

In the metaphysics of presence, then, language is derivative of some essence that precedes it, exerts authority over it. Derivative as it is, however, spoken language has closer affinity to self-presence than does writing, which is itself derivative of speech. In the metaphysics of presence, writing becomes, in effect, a representation of a representation. This attitude toward writing appears quite clearly in Plato's *Phaedrus*, where writing is condemned as that which implants forgetfulness in learners' souls, because they will not use their memories; they will trust to the external written characters and not remember of themselves (275a). Writing is a container of a container, the outside of an outside, a pale reflection of the voice which itself reflects memory—that in-nate (interior and natural) voice which continually tells us the story of our self-presence. Plato's was an important voice in the instauration and maintenance of the metaphysics of presence; thus he makes the textual Socrates complain that writing has no soul, no motivation, no insides; written words may "seem to talk to you as if they were intelligent," but actually "they go on telling you just the same thing forever" (275e).

Throughout the *Grammatology* and other works, Derrida shows how this set of doublings and metaphoric transferences, which privileges mind and self over language, works itself out in the texts of Plato, Aristotle, Jean-Jacques Rousseau, the linguist Ferdinand de Saussure, the anthropologist Claude Lévi-Strauss, Freud, Hegel, Kant, Heidegger, and J. L. Austin, among others. He demonstrates that the metaphysics of presence is a myth, a fiction, a linguistic construct—although it is a construct that is crucial to the maintenance of Western thought, and which is still inscribed in most of our assumptions about human knowledge. Derrida's project, here as elsewhere, is to de-sediment the metaphysical notions that inhere in and surround the important texts of Western culture, to tease out and expose the strands of the metaphysical web from which most of the Western thought is suspended. In other words, he de-constructs the fiction that is metaphysics.

Deconstructive readings of culturally important texts should not be confused with more traditional analytic or critical readings. An analytic reading of a text attempts to establish a meaning for it, to tell other readers what the interpreter thinks the text "means." But to read a text deconstructively is not to produce a doubling commentary, one that would reread the text in order to fix its meaning. Analytic readings cannot escape the deconstructive insight that there is no "meaning," no "ultimate signified" that exists outside the text and to which the text refers or tries to reconstruct. By way of example, Derrida shows that the "characters" which populate Rousseau's *Confessions* are only and necessarily functions of Rousseau's having written the text; that "Rousseau" or Mamma or Theresa have interest and importance only because of their inscription in Rousseau's text. To make the point in

Derrida's words: "in what one calls the real life of these existences "of flesh and bone,' beyond and behind what one believes can be circumscribed as Rousseau's text, there has never been anything but writing" (*OG*, 159).

A deconstructive reading does not try to aim or turn the text toward some overarching system of meaning that would "make sense of it," then. As Derrida remarks, such a reading

> cannot legitimately transgress the text toward something other than it, toward a referent (a reality that is metaphysical, historical, psychobiographical, etc.) or toward a signified outside the text whose content could take place, could have taken place outside of language. (*OG*, 158)

Deconstructive readings do not try to tie a text to some signified that existed prior to and outside of the text (such as Rousseau's "intention" in creating his characters). Rather, such a reading looks for places in the text where a writer's language mis-speaks her, where she loses control of her intention, where she says what she did not "mean" to say. As Derrida puts it, "the reading must always aim at a certain relationship, unperceived by the writer, between what he commands and what he does not command of the patterns of the language that he uses."

Nor are deconstructive readings simply destructive. As Derrida's translator, Barbara Johnson, would have it,

> the deconstructive reading does not point out the flaws or weaknesses or stupidities of an author, but the necessity with which what he does see is systematically related to what he does not see. (*Dis*, xv)

More specifically, Johnson argues that, among other things, a deconstructive reading assumes:

> (1) that the rhetoric of an assertion is not necessarily compatible with its explicit meaning; (2) that this incompatibility can be read as systematic and significant as such; (3) that an inquiry that attempts to study an object by means of that very object is open to certain analyzable aberrations (this pertains to virtually all important investigations: the self analyzing itself, man studying man, thought thinking about thought, language speaking about language, etc.). (xvi)

Deconstruction exposes the dissemination of textual meaning beyond what an author might have intended by trying to tease larger systemic motifs out of gaps, aberrations, or inconsistencies in a given text. It does this because it is aware that language, especially written language, is reflexive rather than representative; it folds back in on itself in very interesting and complex ways which produce meanings that proliferate beyond an author's conscious control.

Let me supply an example of a deconstructive reading that readers of this text can perform for themselves. I am aware, as I write, that there must be blindnesses in my reading of Derrida's texts. These blindnesses necessarily occur because of my own training, my reading habits, my membership in an academic community, and a host of other relationships of which I am only dimly aware. My training and interest in rhetorical theory, for instance, have disposed me toward texts, such as Derrida's, that suspend or question the validity of the sorts of conclusions ordinarily drawn in philosophical discourse. No doubt this disposition operates in such a way that I overlook, or enhance, or diminish, some aspects of Derrida's thought. A deconstructive reading of this text would find those blind spots, and attempt to account for them, not necessarily in terms of its author's biography or ability, or even in terms of the composing situation in which she found herself. Rather, a deconstructive reading would address itself to the blindnesses that are attendant on a given author's residence within any number of cultural or institutional systems, such as the metaphysics of presence or even the English profession.

In "Freud and the Scene of Writing," Derrida describes deconstruction as a double movement, a writing with two hands, that attempts to respect the terms of the conceptual system within which a text was written at the same time as it calls those terms into question (*WD*, 226). Such a reading utilizes the images, structures, references, in a text in a way that respects their inscription there; but it also interrogates those bits of writing in order to see whether, like all language, they also "do their own thing," so to speak. In *Allegories of Reading* (1979), for example, Paul de Man performs a deconstruction of the figure called "rhetorical question," using a text from a popular television series:

> Asked by his wife whether he wants to have his bowling shoes laced over or laced under, Archie Bunker answers with a question: "What's the difference?" Being a reader of sublime simplicity, his wife replies by patiently explaining the difference between lacing over and lacing under, whatever this may be, but provokes only ire. "What's the difference" did not ask for difference but meant instead "I don't give a damn what the difference is." The same grammatical pattern engenders two meanings that are mutually exclusive: the literal meaning asks for the concept (difference) whose existence is denied by the figurative meaning. . . . It is not so that there are simply two meanings, one literal and the other figural, and that we have to decide which one of these meanings

is the right one in this particular situation. The confusion can only be cleared up by the intervention of an extra-textual intention, such as Archie Bunker putting his wife straight; but the very anger he displays is indicative of more than impatience; it reveals his despair when confronted with a structure of linguistic meaning that he cannot control and that holds the discouraging prospect of an infinity of similar future confusions. (9–10)

The confusion surrounding this small text of Archie Bunker's occurs because Ms. Bunker mistakes the context in which Archie asked her to read his remark. In de Man's deconstructive reading, however, Archie has also stumbled onto the fact that a plenitude of meanings resides in language. The implication is that even the reiterated contexts that develop between two people who are married for a long time will not suffice to eliminate the proliferation of meaning toward which language strives. Most telling of all: Ms. Bunker's mistake becomes an occasion for the invention of more discourse, this time about the relative advantages of methods of lacing bowling shoes. As Archie realizes, signifiers have the frustrating property of infinite regeneration.

In one sense, then, deconstruction amounts to reading texts in order to rewrite them. But this rewriting has a different focus than traditional critical reading: Derrida's project, in his early work at least, is to reread Western history in such a way as to give voice to that which has been systematically silenced: that is, to arche-writing, the universal contamination of pure thought by the workings of language. We might say that he wants to expose a fraud, a fraud that has been perpetrated on writing, both in its wider and more literal senses.

Differance and Knowing

Derrida has adopted an important strategy for doing this, which he calls "*differance*." This word is a pun in French, combining the meanings of "differing" (as any set of items lined up in space differ from one another) and "deferring" (as in putting off, delaying). What if (Derrida wonders), what if we assume that the basis of human knowledge does not arise from self-identity, presence, sameness, but rather from difference, from absence? It is the otherness of listeners and readers that gets us talking and writing, after all.

In order to understand how the notion of differance might undo the notions of identity and sameness that underlie the metaphysics of presence, it helps to think of some set of elements that exists in a series—the letters of the alphabet, for example. Any member of the series—the letter "t" for instance—has existence and meaning only insofar as it relates, differentially, to all the other members of the series, such as "i" or "p". Likewise, the word *to* has meaning in English only because it is a member of a sequence or chain of language, all of whose members differ from it: words like *so* and *two* and on and on. We can assign meaning to each term only because we see or hear that its letters or sounds differ from those of its companion; each has meaning only because it belongs to a system of differentiated relationships.

Now, what if this model of differance, as exemplified here in the movement of language, dictates the movement of all human knowledge? That is, what if it is possible to know anything at all only because our knowledge of it differs from our knowledge of other things to which it is related by its context? If we begin to think along these lines, we see that knowledge is both dynamic and contextual. We see, as Vincent Leitch puts it, that "in the realm of knowledge, everything is constituted during a certain time by one or more people. Some 'things' are included, some are excluded, some are marginalized. Boundaries are set up" (1985, 22–23). That is, what a given culture "knows" at a given time is thoroughly historical, even fictitious, in the sense that it is inscribed, written, by and within the culture. Further, this knowledge changes over space and time; its edges change to include new knowledge; what was marginalized becomes central; relations between parts of its internal structure are redefined.

This means, for one thing, that learning is a dynamic process that has no discernible beginning or end. What a culture, or an individual, "knows" at any given moment is available only because its configurations differ from, and yet depend on, what preceded it. This realization points up the futility of establishing spatial or temporal limits or borders around acts of knowing, such as those assumed by labels like "arts and sciences" or "Speech and English" or "theoretical and applied linguistics."

For another thing, a differential model of knowing points up the inter-textual or interrelational aspects of knowing. By way of example: the accidents of one's own life are an important part of the contexts of learning. I could not, would not, have read Derrida but for the accidents of my having had an undergraduate interest in philosophy, a consuming interest in rhetoric, and a friend who spent a year (1977) studying at Yale during the height of excitement there about Derrida's work and who insisted upon his return that I read the *Grammatology* with him. Further, this reading necessarily affected any other reading I undertake: once I read Derrida, I can never again read the writing of other authors (say, Aristotle) in quite the same fashion.[1] And when I re-read Derrida (or re-write him, as I am doing here) in an attempt to understand him "better," it is necessarily true that I only understand him differently.

Additionally, on a differential model of knowing, knowledge is necessarily contextualized: that is, no object of perception can be altogether known when it is studied in isolation from the system that gives it its meaning, from other objects that are both related to it and differ from it, both in space and time. This contextual aspect of inquiry poses a problem with which writers of history are all too familiar: where does one begin, and end, when writing a history of, say, the American Civil War? With the firing of the first shot? With secession? With the institution of slavery? And where does one end? At Appomattox? With Lincoln's assassination? With Reconstruction? And what should the history include—where do its boundaries or margins lie? Within American affairs? Or should the putative interference of other nations also be studied? Should an account of the current cultural scene—journalistic, literary, rhetorical—be included? In short, the dream that objects or events can be isolated from their contexts, that lines or borders can be drawn around them, is another metaphysical fiction.

But the most radical result of tolerating the notion of differance is that it undermines the metaphysical hope of finding what Derrida calls a "transcendental signified." The metaphysics of presence has tried to ignore or halt the movement of differance, to find a stable place to stand outside, or above it, to survey mental and physical landscapes from the vantage point of some solid and non-temporal footing. A variety of candidates for this transcendental footing have been put forward in Western culture: Plato's Ideas, the Judeo-Christian God, empirical reality, the phenomenologists' Subject, Chomsky's deep structures. Metaphysicians want, in short, to establish a signified, a meaning, an essence, that somehow stands outside of the movement of difference—surmounts it, transcends it, conquers it. Empiricists, for example, posit that the evidence given us by our sensations—touch, sight, taste, and the rest—is a pure and entirely trustworthy source of information about the world. Thus they trace the source of meaning, ultimately, to neurological events that they take to be foundational.

Straw Binaries[2]

I have already alluded to the fundamental opposition that entered into the inaugural gesture of metaphysics: inside/outside. Insides—mind, soul, memory—are always preferred to outsides—here the body—

which are somehow fallen, secondary. If we subscribe to the foundational fiction of metaphysics, that minds re-present the world, we also require a series of similar hierarchical oppositions, in which two concepts are unequally pitted against one another, as a way of acknowledging, and yet denying, the movement of differance. For instance: it used to be a commonplace in Catholic theology that Satan's function is to help us to know God, his opposite and superior; we cannot know the good unless we become acquainted with evil. Again, we can discriminate speech from writing only because we have both; their differences from one another help us to understand each more fully. When, however, we privilege one over the other, as the metaphysics of presence privileges the spoken voice over the written text, we try to deny the movement of differance, or at least momentarily to stabilize its movement.

The metaphysics of presence is full of hierarchical oppositions: mind/body, presence/absence, theory/practice, nature/culture, truth/deception, reality/appearance, thought/language, content/form, meaning/expression, literal/figurative. Here is an example of their workings, taken from George Campbell's *Philosophy of Rhetoric* (1776):

> In contemplating a human creature, the most natural division of the subject is the common division into soul and body, or into the living principle of perception and of action, and that system of material organs by which the other receives information from without, and is enabled to exert its powers, both for its own benefit and for that of the species. Analogous to this, there are two things in every discourse which principally claim our attention, the sense and the expression; or in other words, the thought and the symbol by which it is communicated. These may be said to constitute the soul and the body of an oration, or indeed of whatever is signified to another by language. For, as in man, each of these constituent parts hath its distinctive attributes, and as the perfection of the latter consisteth in its fitness for serving the purposes of the former, so it is precisely with those two essential parts of every speech, the sense and the expression. (32)

Here Campbell analogizes the relationship between soul and body to that between thought and expression; both metaphors in turn depend on an inside/outside dichotomy. In both cases, of course, the exterior function (body, language) exists solely to "serve the purposes of the former" (soul, thought). Campbell was not alone among eighteenth-century rhetoricians in employing this conceit, and it found its way into a long-lived American pedagogical tradition that easily and naturally separated "thought" or "content" from "language" or "form"; additionally, the tradition usually privileged the first pair of terms over the second. On this model, "soul" and "thought" are close to originary presence and are thus privileged; they are, quite literally, "insiders," while "body" and "writing" are the "outsiders"— the envelopes or cartons which carry them about and serve their purposes.

Supplementation

All such oppositions contain an interesting irony, however. In the case of speech/writing, for example, metaphysics assumes that writing fills in for, or replaces, speech. As Socrates says, writing "pretends to speak." The irony is that speech, if it is a self-sufficient system of communication, should permit no additions to itself, no supplements.

But speech does have a supplement, precisely, in writing. Further, writing is never content simply to reflect or imitate speech; rather, it pervades and constitutes that for which it substitutes. Derrida argues that the fact of supplementation, the fact that writing can, and does, substitute for speech reminds us, displays to us, differance in operation: it shows that "somewhere, something can be filled up of itself, can accomplish itself, only by allowing itself to be filled through sign and proxy." (*OG*, 145). The supplement, writing, constitutes that which is supplemented. In other words, it isn't until writing exists that speech exists—nothing exists until it is supplemented.

Derrida's critique of supplementation explains why the "art" of classical rhetoric was invented, conceptualized, only when literate skills were widely dispersed among the Greeks. Rhetoric, which is an art of speech, came "into existence," came into consciousness, only when it could be opposed to writing. Yet another example of supplementation came to light in an early 1988 issue of *Esquire* magazine. It was argued there that the generation of Americans known as "yuppies," in the face of the threat posed by the AIDS virus, had replaced sex with money; that is, they had supplemented a biological desire with a culturally induced one, the desire for economic acquisition. Nevertheless, the relation of economics to desire is not an uncomplicated one; it could be argued that the economic system itself stimulates biological desire.

Thus supplementation works in two contradictory ways: it reinforces presence, but it reminds us of its absence, as well:

> The supplement adds itself, it is a surplus, a plenitude enriching another plenitude, the *fullest measure* of presence. It cumulates and accumulates presence. It is thus that art, *techne*, image, representation, convention, etc., come as supplements to nature. . . . But the supplement supplements. It adds only to replace.

> It intervenes or insinuates itself *in-the-place-of*; if it fills, it is as if
> one fills a void. If it represents and makes an image, it is by the
> anterior default of a presence. (*OG*, 144–45)

In Western metaphysics, writing supplements speech (or, more pri-
mordially, speech supplements thought); ideally, the substitutability of
writing for speech reinforces the fullness, the plenitude, of presence.
Writing is yet another system of communication that can do the very
same thing that speech does. But here is the paradox: perversely,
writing never exactly substitutes for speech (or thought); anyone who
has read a transcript of a conversation, or who has tried to compose
a talk-aloud protocol of her writing process, can instantly see this. But
even more profoundly, writing never gets it exactly right; it never
imitates or copies what would be said or thought exactly, but instead
goes off under its own steam, does its own thing. Supplements never
substitute exactly; they always differ from, and defer, realization of
the "real" thing. Think, for example, of the ambivalent attitudes we
have about a photograph of an absent loved one; while the picture
re-minds us of the beloved, its presence also underscores, affirms, his
absence. Thus, the "real thing" is forever "under erasure"; it is both
already there and always not-there.

The Inexhaustibility of Interpretation

In "Signature, Event, Context," Derrida argues that the crucial feature
of written discourse is precisely the author's absence from her text.
Were writers not absent from readers for temporal or geographical
reasons, after all, it would not be necessary for them to write. But
given the necessary absence of authors, writing has the ability to
generate a plenitude of readings or interpretations, a multitude of
meaning. According to Derrida,

> a written sign, in the usual sense of the word, is therefore a mark
> which remains, which is not exhausted in the present of its
> inscription, and which can give rise to an iteration both in the
> absence of and beyond the presence of the empirically determined
> subject who, in a given context, has emitted or produced it. (*MP*,
> 317)

That is, thanks to its author's absence, any piece of writing, even the
smallest scrap, makes itself available to appropriation by readers and
other writers, who can, and do, interpret it in multiple ways.

The author's absence also permits writing to do its work with or without a context: according to Derrida, "it belongs to the sign to be legible . . . even if I do not know what its alleged author-scriptor meant consciously and intentionally at the moment he wrote it, that is abandoned it to its essential drifting" (*MP*, 317). Often readers have no information about the specific context within which writing was composed, but this lack does not keep them from being able to read the text that results. But since any "written sign carries with it a force of breaking with its context, that is, the set of presences which organize the moment of its inscription," any "real" context we might imagine for a text is always constructed by its readers. For example, when we find a scrap of paper with grocery items listed on it lying on the floor of a deserted hallway, we have no immediate way of knowing who its author might be or under what circumstances it was composed. This is not to say, of course, that we cannot read it. But we know only as much about it as our own experience with grocery lists and their uses can supply us. And yet our desire to know what the writing might "mean" is so strong that we can seldom resist the temptation to supply a context for its composition—we suppose we recognize the handwriting, and say to ourselves, "Ah ha! Jones and her family plan to have artichokes for dinner tonight." That is, our desire to construct a stable and specified meaning for texts is so strong that we invent contexts when none are immediately available.[3] Such contexts are sought precisely so that they might ground an (absent) writer's intention, and thus restrain the potential "meanings" of texts from proliferating into infinity.

English teachers are familiar with this process as it works in literary studies; scholars attempt to find out all that can be known about, say, George Eliot's "life and times" in order that we may have a context that will permit us to understand her intention while composing, say, *Middlemarch*. But Derrida would insist that we can never have complete access to Eliot's intentions, as long as we look for these in writing by or about her. Writing, which makes itself available to anyone who can read, never authorizes a given reading all by itself, never tells us exactly what it "means," least of all what its writer's intention might have been. As Derrida remarks in *Dissemination*, "A text is not a text unless it hides from the first comer, from the first glance, the law of its composition and the rules of its game" (63). Any written text may be more or less immediately legible to anyone who is literate in the language in which it is written. This is not to say, however, that a post hoc examination of the circumstances of its composition—its author's intentions, her writing habits, her physical state and the like—will necessarily shed any light on its meaning.

But aside from its break with "external" contexts, another rift characterizes the sign's "semiotic and internal context," according to Derrida. This internal context, any stable formal structure posited for a text, is broken by virtue of its "essential iterability; one can always lift a written syntagma from the interlocking chain in which it is caught or given without making it lose every possibility of functioning, if not every possibility of 'communicating,' precisely" (*MP,* 317). This iterability, or repeatability, of the written sign is what permits it to be cited, grafted into other chains of signs, and harnessed to other uses than the original author may have intended or foreseen (as I have just illustrated by inserting "Derrida's" text into "mine"). But it is also this feature of the written sign, its characteristic "breaking" with its internal context, that compromises its status as "the vehicle, transport, or site of passage of a meaning, and of a meaning that is one" (*MP,* 309). In other words, since written texts can be radically dissociated from their authors' putative intentions, the ability of their internal structure to signal coherent units of "meaning" is also put into serious question. Thus Derrida's work raises doubts about the status of writing as a vehicle for "communication," if this metaphor is to be understood by its association with media that are thought to transmit or "hand over" information, as in "telecommunication." Once again, this is not to say that we cannot read a text. It is simply to observe that the meaning we derive from reading is located as much in the process of reading, and in the social and cultural contexts which surround our reading, as it is in the "text itself."

Whence Grammatology?

Does Derrida's overturning, or underwriting, of Western metaphysics signal the launching of an anti-program, a "positive grammatology," a "science of writing," that would simply invert the hierarchical dichotomies mandated by presence? No. To invert dichotomies, to privilege, say, language over thought, as Plato accused the Sophists of doing, is to be caught, still, within metaphysics once again. Any project aimed at constructing a theory of writing out of Derridean insights is faced at the outset with a major difficulty. There is grave doubt whether the study of writing may be the sort of "positive science" around which theories can evolve.

In the *Grammatology* Derrida struggles with his realization that

> a science of writing runs the risk of never being established as
> such and with that name. Of never being able to define the unity
> of its project or its object. Of not being able either to write its
> discourse on method or to describe the limits of its field. (4)

Any alternative to Western metaphysics is necessarily bound within
the tradition that makes alternatives thinkable: as Derrida remarks,
the "fundamental condition" of a grammatology "is certainly the
undoing of logocentrism. But this condition of possibility turns into a
condition of impossibility," since "one must know *what* writing *is* in
order to ask—knowing what one is talking about and what *the question
is*—where and when writing begins" (*OG*, 74–75). The dilemma is
this: to raise questions about the nature of writing is to ask questions
about its historicity and origin, questions that (can) be given empirical
answers, and that are irrevocably bound up with questions about
essences and thus with the metaphysics of presence.

Derrida argues that the "otherness" which founds writing in opposition to speech accounts for the fact that the scholarly study of
writing has amounted to re-constructing its history, for the most part.
Even though "all the great histories of writing open with an exposition
of a classificatory and systematic project," no such typology has ever
succeeded in making satisfactory distinctions among hieroglyphic,
pictographic, ideographic, syllabic, or alphabetic scripts.[4] No matter
how these distinctions are made, some script or scripts always leak
through the cracks, cross the lines, their characters now acting like
hieroglyphs, now like pictograms. Derrida locates the theoretical in-
sufficiency of histories of writing in

> the false evidence that guides the work. Evidence all the more
> efficacious because it belongs to the deepest, the oldest, and
> apparently the most natural, the least historical layer of our
> conceptuality, that which best eludes criticism, and especially
> because it supports that criticism, nourishes it, and informs it; our
> historical ground itself. (*OG*, 81–82).

That is, to construct a theory of writing that would undo its heretofore
silent role in history, to give a voice to writing, as it were, would be
to undo history itself. Such a move cannot (yet) be thought.

Nonetheless, the Western habit of opposing thought to writing can
be foregrounded and interrogated. At the very least such an interrogation sheds light on the intellectual conditions under which most
teachers of reading and writing do their work.

2 Deconstruction and the English Profession

In the 1970s, a group of literary critics at Yale University introduced American readers to Derrida's work. Thanks to the many books and papers circulated by the so-called "Yale critics"—Paul de Man, J. Hillis Miller, and Geoffrey Hartman, among others—deconstruction (or at least its American version) has since become a recognizable school of literary thought in this country. The intrusion of deconstruction into the genteel industry that is American literary criticism initially caused something of an uproar. And, because of its emphasis on writing, teachers and theorists of composition also responded to the entry of deconstruction onto the American critical scene. This chapter reviews those reactions, and tries to account for some of the responses made by English teachers toward deconstruction.

Traditional critics were pretty much agreed that a deconstructive approach to the reading of literary texts was either trivial or (paradoxically enough) dangerous. The first important skirmish between proponents of the older and newer schools of critical thought took place in the late 1970s, when M. H. Abrams defended "traditional historians of Western culture" against a perceived attack on them by Yale critic J. Hillis Miller. Abrams listed the "essential premises" that motivated traditional criticism as follows:

1. The basic materials of history are written texts; and the authors who wrote these texts (with some off-center exceptions) exploited the possibilities and norms of their inherited language to say something determinate, and assumed that competent readers, insofar as these shared their own linguistic skills, would be able to understand what they said.

2. The historian is indeed for the most part able to interpret not only what the passages that he cites might mean now, but also what their writers meant when they wrote them. Typically, the historian puts his interpretation in language which is partly his author's and partly his own; if it is sound, this interpretation approximates, closely enough for the purpose at hand, what the author meant.

3. The historian presents his interpretation to the public in the expectation that the expert reader's interpretation of a passage will approximate his own and so confirm the "objectivity" of his interpretation. (1977, 426)

In other words, traditional historians of culture, like traditional literary critics, assumed that written texts contained some determinable coherent meaning, which had been put there in accordance with an author's discernible intention (that is, the author's intention could be discerned when the text was read by someone else). They further assumed that "expert" readers of the same text would find similar meanings in it. This assumption in turn guaranteed the critics' certainty that meaning was somehow "objective," that it was embodied in the text in such a way that any sensitive reader could ferret it out.

Thus Abrams assumed that an authoritative reading could be made for a literary text—a reading which would put a stop to all other readings and which would, then, not itself be readable (that is, open to criticism). Abrams wanted to establish stable and unassailable interpretations for literary texts, thus assuming, from a deconstructive point of view, that they enjoyed some special existence outside the movement of differance. On Abrams's textual model, since transcendental meanings ought to be found for important texts, arguments about its meaning indicated that one of the parties to the dispute was somehow misreading or misunderstanding the text at hand.

On the other hand, Abrams argued, deconstructive critics like Miller accepted an entirely different set of notions about texts; they assumed that there is no correct interpretation of a text, and further, that texts authorize innumerable interpretations. Abrams concluded that deconstructive approaches to texts negate the possibility that critics, or any readers, can ever understand a text or each other's readings of the same text. While Abrams's account of deconstructive tenets is fair enough, the conclusions he draws—that deconstructive approaches to texts negate the possibility that critics or readers can ever understand a text or each other's readings of the same text—are inaccurate. On a deconstructive model of textuality, literary texts do not hold still and docilely submit themselves to repeated identical readings; they can be read and reread, and each reading differs from the last. Nor are critical interpretations of texts copies of an original "meaning" that is somehow housed in the original text. Interpretations, readings, differ from the texts they interpret and from each other; and, having been read, they require a re-reading of the "originary" text. This is why critical readings of important texts can continue to be made, why the pages of *PMLA* will always be filled up.

In 1979 Murray Krieger identified these and other post-structural claims about texts as major threats to the institutionalized study of literature.[1] He began by arguing that "these recent theoretical notions, by their very nature, have little or no interest in improving our capacity for literary analysis" (32). That is, post-structural readings of texts are quite unlike readings done according to the "new criticism"—readings that explicate, analyze, and interpret literary texts as though the context in which they were produced is irrelevant and as though their internal structures yield up sufficient clues to their interpretation. (New critical readings produce articles and books with titles like "Blood and Roses: Symbol and Structure in Hawthorne's Short Fiction.") Unlike new critics, deconstructive critics were emphatically not interested in producing more critical commentaries that aimed at taking literary texts apart in order to decide what they meant. Nor were they particularly interested in establishing single, authoritative readings for canonical texts.

However, Krieger correctly discerned that post-structural notions about texts posed a serious threat to the new critical assumption that "literary discourse is a significant variant of discourse at large." That is to say, post-structural notions about the nature of written discourse call into question the traditional assumption that literary discourse is somehow special, that (in Krieger's words) "the literary work is created as such through deviations from 'normal discourse' that are manipulated into an object that manifests its full and totalizing presence" (1979, 32). Like more traditional critics, Krieger assumed that the formal features of literary discourse, which are somehow superior to, and different from, those used in "ordinary" (non-literary) discourse, endowed literature with some special qualities of completeness, fullness, and self-sufficiency. Of course, it is precisely the assumption that literary discourse is more "real" or "enduring" than other sorts of discourse that has enabled English departments to grow and flourish.

Radical critics also found reasons to dismiss deconstruction. Despite its perceived threat to the literary establishment, deconstruction was denounced by leftist critics who saw it as "politically bankrupt," since it contained no theory of social change and offered no program for altering the status quo. Radical critics mounted the same critique against deconstruction as they had against new criticism—neither critical program, they argued, had any built-in facility for immersing literary texts in the political and cultural contexts which shape them, and on which they comment. The only difference between deconstruction and new criticism, as far as many radical critics could see, was that deconstruction's incipient critique of determinate meaning seemed more daring, more risky, than did the traditional critic's clinging to textual objectivity. As Marxist critic Terry Eagleton put it, "deconstruction is as disorienting in North America as it was for Mrs. Moore in India; it thus provides you with all the risks of a radical politics while cancelling the subject who might be summoned to become an agent of them" (1981, 139). Eagleton seems to imply here that the concept of a self-motivated actor is requisite to any theory or pragmatics of social action.

Radical teachers and critics were especially disappointed by the "received standard version" of deconstruction that evolved in American departments of English thanks to the influence of the Yale critics. In their hands, the radicals argued, deconstruction had become only a slick disguise for new criticism, all dressed up in a new language. As Michael Ryan put it, the Yale school translated "a complex philosophy into an old-model new criticism from which the muffler has been removed, creating more noise without noticeably improving the speed."[2] This perceived devolution of deconstructive thought into just another critical approach has lent force to the analyses of those critics who now say that its advent onto the American critical scene simply "makes no difference" (to borrow from the title of a book by Michael Fischer).

Deconstruction had its defenders, of course, in the Yale critics and those they influenced. Such persons hailed deconstructive thought as the solution to the intellectual stagnation in which literary criticism was mired after its wholesale adoption of the new criticism in the 1950s and 1960s. In the late 1970s, J. Hillis Miller articulated a deconstructive attitude toward traditional critical thought. Such work, he contended, tended to "freeze into a quasi-scientific discipline promising exhaustive rational certainty in the identification of meaning in a text and in the identification of the way that meaning is produced" (Hartman 1979, 249). Miller cited an essay by Abrams, who had suggested (according to Miller) that texts have, or ought to have, an "obvious and univocal" reading. Miller argued that no such readings were possible. The only reading that could be truly "univocal," after all—one which could speak with only one voice—would simply replace the original text; the authority of the critical work would obviate the need to read the literary work it interpreted. Because this is the case, Miller said, "criticism is a human activity which depends for its validity on never being at ease within a fixed 'method.' It must constantly put its own grounds in question" (Hartman 1979, 249). For Miller, as well as for many other critics, deconstruction offered them the most fruitful and rigorous means of putting their own methods into question, and thus of producing richer and more self-aware readings of literary texts.

Indeed, in an impressive series of works published during the 1970s, Miller, de Man, Hartman and company demonstrated that deconstructive approaches to major texts yielded new and exciting insights about them.

People who are interested in composition and its teaching have also responded to post-structural theory, but the debate over it in those circles has been carried on with much less intensity than among literary critics. In an essay published in *College Composition and Communication* in 1984, Edward White conjectured that post-structural thought had enjoyed a more congenial reception from writing teachers than it had from literary critics, because, rather than threatening any well-established foundations, post-structural notions about language were comfortably compatible with much recent speculation in composition theory:

> These reading theories thus provide even more substantial theoretical justification for reacting to student writing as if it were part of a process. . . . There is a fundamental ground of practical good sense in contemporary literary theory that helps us understand why the best of us teach the way we do, and why we have so much trouble communicating writing theory to our colleagues for whom the New Criticism is still new. (187)

Here White noticed the consonance of post-structural notions of textuality with those that are bound up, if only implicitly, in "process pedagogy."

Other writing teachers have found that deconstruction offers some useful grounds from which to initiate critiques of traditional writing instruction. For example, Susan Miller (1982) has written a convincing deconstructive reading of the curious status of textbooks in composition instruction, and J. Hillis Miller (1983) put deconstruction to work in order to disassemble the set of restrictive notions about metaphor which appear in traditional composition textbooks.

Other composition teachers have used deconstructive notions in a more generative fashion. In an essay entitled "Making Differences in the Composition Class: A Philosophy of Invention," William Covino demonstrated how deconstructive notions support and reinforce composition teachers' assumption that invention is an important part of the writing process. As he remarked, writing teachers

> must connect literacy, understood as the power to use language appropriately and effectively, with Invention, which must be understood as the unifying term for the whole process of composition. Jacques Derrida's post-structuralist stance commands our attention, because it signals a new appreciation for playful invention as the very center and circumference of all language. (1981, 1)

Of course, a deconstructive pedagogy would locate invention within the movement of language itself, rather than in the individual writer, as much current composition theory does.

But deconstruction has not enjoyed unalloyed success among writing teachers and composition theorists. In 1986, Jon Harned dismissed deconstruction out of hand, arguing that it is too esoteric for the workaday needs of writing teachers. Like traditional literary critics, Harned saw that deconstruction challenges some basic assumptions about writing instruction. Nevertheless he minimized the potential impact of deconstructive analyses on composition instruction by arguing that writing teachers are not "likely to be convinced" by the post-structural "attempt to make everything disappear into a haze of language" (14). And rhetorician Ross Winterowd wrote off deconstruction as a potential source of writing theory, initially because Derrida's own texts are difficult (1983). But Winterowd further characterized Derrida's theorizing as dillettante, if not downright anti-social, classing it with a vulgarized version of Romanticism known as "vitalism" (1987, 269).

The Role of Theory in Teaching Reading and Writing

One of my colleagues recently sent me a news clipping recounting a discussion that had taken place at a meeting of literary critics. According to the clipping, which I paraphrase, the respected literary critic who had given the keynote address at the meeting announced that "deconstruction is dead on both coasts." A member of the audience promptly regretted the death of deconstruction at Yale and Berkeley, avowing that deconstruction was at least alive and well in Oklahoma. With that, a third member of the audience accounted for its death on the coasts by noting that "deconstruction is stalled in Cincinnati."

I recount this anecdote partly to introduce the theme of this chapter of my essay and partly to justify my continuing interest in deconstruction, despite the fact that it has been pronounced dead at some institutions of higher learning. My theme here is simply that adherence to any theory within English departments is partly a matter of politics; one's choice of a theoretical stance dictates not only one's teaching practices but also bears an important relationship to one's status within the English profession. This is as true of adherents to more traditional theories of reading and writing as it is of those who have adopted post-structuralist positions.

Despite official announcements of their demise, deconstruction and post-structuralism have affected the politics of American departments of English in fundamental ways. In many colleges and universities, literary theory has become a more respectable teaching interest than it once was, and university teachers can now be hired because they are "theorists" or "deconstructionists" or "post-structuralists" rather than "Miltonists" or "Chaucerians." And, as White (1984) noted, the new emphasis on literary theory is congenial, in many respects, with the recent growth of interest in rhetoric and composition theory, fields whose assumptions about language are sometimes compatible with those made in post-structural thought.

Despite these developments, post-structuralism, and especially that branch of it called "deconstruction," is still more heard about than read and more notorious than respected. I suspect that the clamor that surrounds deconstruction is often a product of simple or willful misunderstanding of its program and of its pedagogical and political potential.[3] But the cacophony of voices that surrounds deconstruction might also be taken as testimony to its fertility for rethinking the nature of literary criticism, as well as the pedagogies that are traditionally used in teaching reading and writing.

A while back, I attended a lecture given by a distinguished literary critic who performed a perceptive, charming, and persuasive reading of some aspects of poet Wallace Stevens's life and work. In a subsequent talk, the critic argued that the aim of all literary pedagogy should be to politicize students—to make them aware, as far as possible, that they and their culture subscribe to a number of constraining ideologies regarding class, sex, and race. Since I am in sympathy with his proposal, I asked him, in the discussion session that followed, exactly how he went about accomplishing the politicization of his students, in his classroom, every day. How, for example, would he incorporate his brilliant reading of Stevens's perplexity about questions of gender into a course in American literature? The critic was reluctant to answer my question and even seemed embarrassed for me. He apparently thought that by asking him for a lesson plan, or an account of what he does on Monday, I was demeaning myself (and him, by implication). At least a member of the audience rescued both of us from the embarrassing impasse that ensued by asking another question.

I recount this anecdote because I want to illustrate a bifurcation that is currently at work within the English teaching profession. I refer, of course, to the bifurcation between theory and practice. It is possible, these days, to speak both of "reading theory" and "writing theory"; both activities are currently undergoing scrutiny on a level that can only be called "theoretical." The act of reading has recently been radically redefined by theorists such as Wolfgang Iser, Stanley Fish, and Jane Tompkins; such thinkers view reading as a constructive act wherein readers recreate texts while they read them. Writing is also the subject of a good deal of current theoretical speculation; while philosophers like Derrida and Richard Rorty are studying its uniqueness as a kind of language use, cognitive psychologists are investigating the process by which people produce it.

But reading and writing are also practices that are widely employed in society at large. More, they are practices whose ubiquity lends support to yet another kind of practice: they are taught in school. Most students who matriculate from any institution of learning in America have studied both from the time they were able to manage either. Nevertheless, as my anecdote about the literary critic illustrates, the practice of reading pedagogy (called "teaching literature" in English departments) is generally "occulted," as deconstructive critics say, at least after students leave elementary school. The practice of teaching people to read difficult and culturally influential texts is carried on, for the most part, as though it were innocent of theory, as though it were a knack that anyone could pick up by practicing it.

But such work is manifestly not innocent of theory; no one who thinks much about such matters can doubt that new critical assumptions about the nature of texts inform a good deal of current literary pedagogy.[4] In 1984, William Cain noted that "New Critical attitudes, values, and emphases" are "so deeply ingrained in English studies . . . that we do not even perceive them as the legacy of a particular movement" (105). Rather, Cain argued, the new criticism

> has been transformed into "criticism," the essence of what we do as teachers and critics. . . . its lessons about literary study lead a vigorous life, setting the norms for effective teaching and marking the boundaries within which nearly all criticism seeks to validate itself. It is the New Criticism that defines and gives support to the central job of work that we perform: "practical criticism," the "close reading" of literary texts. "Close reading" forms the substance of most critical essays and books, and it is reinforced in our classrooms, where we teach verbal analysis to students. (1984, 105)

And if the new criticism informs most literary pedagogy, it has also exerted a powerful influence on writing instruction. Since many teachers of writing were trained to be teachers of literature, and have no training in composition at all, it is only natural that they transfer the set of assumptions made about texts in new criticism into their teaching of composition.

If I am right about this, teachers of literature who were trained in new critical approaches to literary texts, if they are consistent, must inevitably transfer their thinking about such texts to the student-authored texts they read. That is, such persons will think of student texts as the finished products of their authors' coherent and determinable intention. They will assume further that an analysis of the text's structure and content should reveal some coherent meaning, and should give some clue to its author's intention. Such teachers will also assume that their reading of such texts is authoritative, given their expert status as readers. They further assume that the meaning they discern on the page has some "objective" status. Thus the student authors of such texts ought to be able to see the meaning (or lack thereof) that their teachers see in a completed paper.

Another set of textual assumptions, whose tenets are in many ways compatible with those of the new criticism, has also been brought to bear in writing instruction. Until 1970 or so, many teachers of writing subscribed, consciously or not, to a discernible and coherent theory of composition, now known as "current-traditional rhetoric." This theory dictates that texts should be thought of as products of a writer's coherent intention; that the presence of ill- or well-formed formal features in texts (sentences, paragraphs, thesis statements) is indicative of the quality of the writer's thought; that texts can or ought to be composed within a number of formal generic constraints ("expressive"; "expository"), and so on. Most composition teachers assimilated current-traditional thought from their own teachers or from textbooks. And, like new criticism in literary pedagogy, the traditional model is still very much alive in writing instruction, influencing course design, textbook selection, choice of preferred genres, and the nature of assignments.

Aside from their possible subscription to these two more or less occulted theories of textuality, most teachers of writing have had access to very little writing theory. Until quite recently, in fact, most of what was known about teaching writing was an accretion of practical lore, built up over time within the community of its practitioners. As Stephen North argues in *The Making of Knowledge in Composition* (1987), "practice clearly . . . remains now, not only a distinguishable mode of inquiry, but the one most widely pursued in the field" (22). North characterizes the "lore" generated by practitioners as having several characteristics, among the most notable of which is its imperviousness to fully rationalized critique. Lore is absolutely inclusive: according to North,

> literally anything can become a part of lore. The only requirement for entry is that the idea, notion, practice, or whatever be nominated: some member of the community must claim that it worked, or seemed to work, or might work. (24)

Too, nothing that has gained admission is ever dropped from lore, even though some of its tenets might in this way become contradictory: " 'Know what you want to say before you begin to write.' 'Write in order to find out what you want to say.' 'Never use the first person.' 'It's perfectly all right to use the first person.' " North's examples of potential contradiction point up the hazards of grounding the teaching of writing in practitioner lore.

A teacher's subscription to any theory of textuality influences nearly all of the decisions he makes when teaching reading and writing. And if his subscription to this or that theory has not been carefully articulated, he is liable to confuse his students in fundamental ways. For example, if a practitioner accepts recent lore concerning "process pedagogy," but has not altogether rejected traditional composition theory, it will be difficult for him to discern whether his particular combination of the two pedagogies entails contradictions or confusions.

Because of the properties of practitioner lore, which has no mechanism for rejecting incompatible theories or strategies, this teacher is not encouraged to inquire whether the two pedagogical models— current-traditional and writing-as-process—conflict in serious ways. Unless he theorizes about these matters, he will not be able to determine whether his new emphasis on writing-as-process fits comfortably within the traditional understanding that texts exist inside identifiable generic categories (exposition, argumentation, the "personal essay" and so on). Does the task of writing produce a continuous flow of discourse, or ought written texts to emerge from writers' pens in such a way as to conform to identifiable generic and structural requirements? If the two notions are in conflict, such a teacher risks confusing his students (and himself) on a fundamental level.

As should be obvious by now, I think that reading and writing pedagogies are inevitably grounded in theory, whether these theories are consciously subscribed to or not. If a pedagogical strategy is to be coherent, then, its teachers must articulate its rationale for themselves as fully as possible. Such a fully articulated rationale will explain why one strategy may be preferred to another; more, it will help teachers to understand the ideological ramifications of their teaching strategies. To subscribe to current-traditional rhetoric, for example, is to adopt its positivist underpinnings, with all that entails about the methodical movement of thought and the representative role of language.[5]

Like the new criticism and current-traditional rhetoric, deconstruction is a theory of textuality. Unlike them, however, its ramifications for the processes of reading and writing have been carefully articulated by Derrida and his commentators. But deconstruction is also a practice, and this practice is performed and illustrated, over and over, in Derrida's writing. This analytic, or critical, feature of deconstruction renders it particularly interesting for teachers of reading and writing. On the theoretical level, deconstruction provides a relatively coherent description of the nature of texts and textuality, a description whose tenets should help us to verify the coherence of any models of the writing process we construct. On the level of critique, deconstruction should do for traditional writing instruction what it does for texts: it can provide a means of reading current classroom techniques in such a way as to expose their strengths and deficiencies.

3 Deconstructing Writing Pedagogy

Deconstruction, and its concern with metaphysics, minds, and the history of Western philosophy may seem so esoteric as to be far removed from the needs of the classroom teacher of English. I don't think that this is the case, however. Aside from its intrinsic interest, deconstruction harbors a number of important implications for the teaching of English. For one thing, it presents some interesting models for reading and studying literary texts (and student texts as well), models which might be profitably emulated in reading or writing pedagogy. For another, deconstructive insights about teaching, language, and writing offer up a critique on which we can hang much of the pedagogical practice that has been adopted by writing teachers in recent years.

However, a deconstructive reading of English teaching carries with it a good many negative implications, insofar as it calls into question some of the basic assumptions that have always taken for granted in such teaching.[1] For example, a deconstructive analysis undermines the notion that the composing process begins with an originating author; this notion characterizes both traditional and process pedagogies of composition. Deconstruction also rejects the traditional characterization of writing as a repetition of the same (as is now the case with instruction in expository writing, which is supposed to re-present— picture, imitate, copy—some piece of a student's knowledge). Such an analysis also challenges the notion that informs and permeates traditional pedagogy: that language is a transparent representation of the world and/or of the minds which populate it.

Reassuringly enough, a deconstructive reading of writing pedagogy underscores the appropriateness of much of the lore connected with process pedagogy. It also demonstrates, however, that some alterations remain to be considered, if we take deconstructive notions about language seriously. But challenges like these can strengthen a tradition that survives them. As Vincent Leitch has remarked with regard to Derrida's own engagement with pedagogical issues, to threaten a system of beliefs is also to "foster inquiry and transformation" (1985, 18).

Sovereignty and Authority

As I tried to establish earlier in this essay, post-structural thought raises serious objections to the metaphysical fiction that would place a sovereign, self-aware consciousness at the center of any composing act. I don't think it is unfair to say that traditional thinking about writing has been author-centered, and that, as a consequence, writing pedagogy has always focused on authors—specifically on their intentions and psychology. Apparently, the view that the writing process begins and ends with an individual author is a historical phenomenon whose ubiquity in modern thought has to do with attitudes toward discourse that were developed during the seventeenth century.[2] This attitude still prevails in our thinking, although post-structuralist historians have begun to question its staying power.

In our own time, the author-centeredness of writing pedagogy has given rise to a school of research into composing that studies the mental habits of composers. These researchers are trying to devise a model of the composing process that is supposed to reflect the composing process used by all writers. They draw on cognitive psychology for their rationale and techniques, assuming that this discipline which studies "the human mind" can provide us a key to understanding the nature of writing.

But the assumption that authorial minds are solely responsible for the production of written texts is also held by composition theorists who are not explicitly tied to cognitivist models. In many cases, the author-centeredness of their theories of composition derives from their unwitting subscription to the metaphysics of presence. For example, C. H. Knoblauch and Lil Brannon append the following footnote to the opening chapter of their *Rhetorical Traditions and the Teaching of Writing*:

> Composing is a richer concept than "writing" and wherever we use the term we mean to designate the forming/shaping activities of mind, not merely the learned behaviors associated with writing in the narrowest sense—using a pen or pencil, making the letters of written discourse, using the technical conventions of the written language, and so on. The distinction is crucially important because "composing" is a natural human endowment while "writing" is learned. Yet writing means next to nothing if divorced from the larger concept of "composing." (1984, 19–20)

To a reader who is alert to the deconstructive directions taken by language, this comment is reminiscent of the traditional canard that "thinking" (here called "composing") precedes writing. Not only that, thinking is better than writing, since the former takes place in an author's mind, while writing takes place in language. "Composing" is "natural" for Knoblauch and Brannon, but writing is not; writing is artificial, foreign, monstrous, almost meaningless, an unnatural act. Writing is not self-sufficient on this model; rather it is a technology that depends for its value on some other process which is more essentially human, more present to itself.

The post-structural critique of the notion of the sovereign self poses a number of difficulties for a research program, or a pedagogy, centered on the psychology of authors. As Derrida points out in the *Grammatology*, psychology can only survive by positing a "naturalist opposition" between "internal" and "external" experience. The difficulty is that, on a psychological model, writing is, stubbornly, an "exteriority"; we will never be able to account for writing by looking for some "interiority" that exists above or beyond or in back of it. Even if students of the composing process find a research technique that permits them to establish a model of the writing process which describes, in the most minute physiological or psychological detail, what happens in the minds or brains of people who write, we will nevertheless have learned nothing about the uses to which writers put language, which by definition is never private. And if psychologists or psycholinguists succeed in finding or describing some mechanism that accounts for the production of language, they will not have made much progress toward grasping the nature of writing, the uses of which depend on its availability to the community that is served and defined by it.

Further, since writing is made up of language, it both precedes and succeeds individual writers. Thus a deconstructive attitude toward writing pedagogy will focus its attention away from individual authors and toward the language currently in use in the community served by the pedagogy.

Because of both its implicit critique of the sovereign self and its emphasis on the absence of readers from the composing act, deconstructive attitudes toward language allow us to redefine many of the crucial terms with which we work every day—terms like "reader" and "writer." In a review of Derrida's *The Post Card* (1984), Gayatri Spivak argues that the "scene of writing" (what composition theorists call the "composing process") requires absence as its necessary condition. That is, the scene of writing denies the sovereign authorial presence so often invoked by traditional pedagogy. Spivak notes that "when a man writes, he is in a structure that needs his absence as its necessary condition (writing is defined as that which can necessarily be read in the writer's absence)" (1984, 19). That is, when (if) a writer writes, he does so because the desired audience is not immediately present. Its "presence," if you will, is fictional; it "exists" only insofar as the writer imaginatively embodies it, as some construct of future reader(s).

What is even more curious, the scene of writing thus mandates the writer's pluralization; for the duration of composing, writer becomes audience, a move that must be made in order for there to be a motive for writing at all. Spivak argues that writers resist this pluralization of themselves, and that readers conspire with them by assuming that the discourse has been produced by a writing "self": as she puts it,

> when a person reads, the scene of writing is usually ignored and the argument is taken as the product of a self with a proper name. Writers and readers are thus accomplices in the ignoring of the scene of writing. (20)

This misperception of the act of writing is enhanced by the installment of writing between the covers of papers, books, and anthologies, whose white margins allow readers to think the writing "contained" therein is complete, and more, that it represents the completed thought of the person whose name is attached to them. When readers read, then, they are seduced by textual artifacts into believing that the text was composed by an integrated "self," who possessed a unified "intention," and who carried out that intention with more or less success. In other words, they assume that the written discourse somehow re-presents the "thoughts" or "intentions" of its "writer."

But the Derridean critique of the inability of selves to "re-present" themselves in language demonstrates that all of this is yet another metaphysical construct. As Jasper Neel explains,

> most Western writers assume that writing serves as a vehicle to carry thought. But this assumption remains forever haunted by the problem that thinking (at least in the Western sense of thinking) cannot appear outside writing. Something at the core of thinking seems to be missing. Writing adds what is missing but in doing so reveals the incompleteness of the thing that needs a supplement to be itself. . . . This process of supplementation endangers thought because writing, rather than merely serving as an empty vehicle waiting to transport and then discharge thought whole, adds itself to and then substitutes itself for thought. (1988, 162)

What readers read is writing, not thought.

And yet the fiction of authorial sovereignty is lent enormous force by the power relationship that is inherent in all writing, when seen from the writer's point of view.[3] The solitude that often accompanies the act of writing seduces writers into believing that they are engaged in individual acts of creation; it is all too easy to forget, while writing, that one's language belongs to a community of speakers and writers, that one has begun writing in order to reach (absent) readers, and that one's "innovative ideas" have long textual histories behind them, histories which contain many many voices. Think, for example, of the voices that speak throughout this writing: Derrida's, of course, but also Jasper Neel's, Aristotle's, Gayatri Spivak's, Meyer Abrams's, Barbara Johnson's, and on and on.

Because of the illusion of authorial sovereignty, it is difficult for writers to acknowledge the inevitable immersion of their own voices in the flow of differance. Two groups are excepted from this generalization. The first consists of experienced writers, who have learned throughout many trials the difficulty of getting readers to "see" what was "meant." Over time these writers have learned to assume the point of view of potential readers, whose voices are always being heard during the writing process (in the back of the head, so to speak). Such writers produce "readerly" prose, and can carry on an imagined dialogue with potential readers as they compose. In other words, experienced writers know how to submit themselves to the flow of the community's language. The second group consists of inexperienced writers, who find their own voices simply drowned out by those of teachers and other sources of discursive authority. In a sense, then, inexperienced writers are more in touch with the flow of differance than are writers who accept the fiction of authorial sovereignty.

Assuming a deconstructive perspective, then, I must argue that to center a writing pedagogy on authors, rather than on readers and the common language of the community, is to insert an attitude into the composing act that misunderstands its focus. I would argue further that traditional composition pedagogy begins from the notion of authorship, not only because of its immersion in the metaphysics of presence, but also because the teachers who design such courses are writers whose work commands a good deal of authority, while their students are only readers, at least within the confines of the writing classroom.

Ironically enough, teachers do most of the writing in composition classes—they write the syllabus, the assignments, and the daily lesson plans; they re-write the textbook in the sense that they interpret it for their students; and finally, they write (revise, edit, grade) their students' papers. Students, on the other hand, spend most of their time reading: they read the teacher, to determine what he "wants"; they read the textbooks or anthologies he has assigned to find out what he wants them to know; they read his assignments to determine what he wants them to do. When they "write" in response to his assignments, they tell him what they think he wants to hear and write according to the rules he wants to see realized in their papers. Almost never do they envision themselves as having something to teach their teachers.

As teachers, it is all too easy for us to be seduced into acting as the only writers of/in a writing course, to refuse students the opportunity to wrest that role from us. And it is even easier for students to accept the role of perpetual reader, inasmuch as they have been invited to do just this throughout most of their school lives. And yet to do so is to ignore the movement of writing, of differance, that always postpones the achievement of final authority for discourse. Deconstruction assumes the complicitly of writers and readers in all acts of composing. That is, readers of any discourse become its writers as they re-construct a "meaning" for it.

If writing teachers find this argument compelling, there are some strategies available to them. They can reject or redefine some of the traditional strategies that implicitly reinforce their power as writers of the composition course. One of these is the notion of intention. As William Covino remarks, if we accept deconstructive notions about writing,

> all writing takes place without finality because finality is located in some sort of definition or purpose. . . . We may suspect that our insistence as teachers upon "writing with a purpose" deserves questioning insofar as it subordinates "strategy without finality" to "the self-assured certitude of consciousness." (1981, 2)

At the very least, any pedagogy which insists that students' papers reflect "the self-assured certitude of consciousness" must contradict the daily experience of writing teachers. A deconstructive pedagogy, on the other hand, would redirect the notion of intention or purpose away from examination of a text and onto its suitability to the rhetorical situation for which it was designed. Perhaps it would even reject the notion of intention altogether and substitute the task of incorporating the projected needs of audiences into the writing process.

A deconstructive analysis begins by assuming that writing is communal, that, as Michael Ryan puts it, "writing can belong to anyone; it puts an end to the ownership or self-identical property that speech signaled" (1982, 29). The failure of writing to signal its ownership by anyone is, of course, exactly why Plato's Socrates condemned it:

> Once a thing is put in writing, the composition, whatever it may be, drifts all over the place, getting into the hands not only of

those who understand it, but equally of those who have no business with it; it doesn't know how to address the right people, and not address the wrong. (275e)

It may be misguided as well as uncharitable of me to charge Plato with hierarchizing the reading public here, but it seems unmistakable that he wanted to reserve the use of writing for those who understood its power. Apparently he detested or feared the democratic tendency of writing, its insistence on making itself available to any who can read.

The public nature of writing, its refusal to be possessed by either writer or reader, works itself out in several interesting ways. First of all, it supports the notion recently advanced by some composition theorists that all writing is collaborative. Research into the production of writing in the marketplace has established that most of this sort of work is the product of many hands.[4] It is also the case, however, that much writing for which authors take individual credit is, in fact, collaborative. By way of illustration, I repeat a story told by Tilly Warnock, a teacher of writing:

> One cold July night several years ago at Vedauwoo, during the Wyoming Conference on Freshman and Sophomore English, several people were talking beside the fire when one man began explaining how exhausted he was from revising his textbook. We asked how he writes. He described his writing process in detail but seemed particularly pleased with the stage when he passes his draft to his wife, who is not in English, so that she can detect the b.s. in his work. Because I was delighted by his account, I asked if he included such collaboration as a common stage for writers in his textbook. He drew himself to full height, a large shadow against the flames and silhouettes of the mysteriously shaped mountains, and replied indignantly, "Every word I write is my own." The conversation ended. (1985, 305)

Such husband-wife collaborations are no doubt numerous; many are acknowledged, however, only in prefaces or dedications that thank spouses for their "unfailing patience and dedication to the manuscript." One also wonders about the role of Milton's daughters in the composition of *Paradise Lost*, the women who "recorded" the poem while the blind poet dictated. Other, silent collaborators are editors, only a few of whom, like Maxwell Perkins (who fashioned Thomas Wolfe's chaotic manuscripts into readable novels), are ever credited for the writing they do on a text. From a Derridean point of view, editorship of a work-in-progress, or any reading of it, counts as part of its writing. This is equally true for the writing classroom. Thus the students who read their colleagues' works-in-progress and comment on them are as much a part of their composition as is the "original" author; this is true of teacherly readings as well.

Indeed, even from a single "originary" writer's point of view, the instigation of writing simply cannot be isolated from its contexts, which are myriad. They include not only the writer, her sense of her present state and her memory of her past; they include her attitude toward the present assignment, her teacher, her class, the other students in it, toward schooling in general and her schooling in particular, her past experiences with writing and with writing classes and assignments. They also include her physical state at the time of writing, and the tools she uses; and perhaps less obviously they include her role in, and attitude toward, the communities of which she is a part—her family, her friends, her neighborhood, ghetto or barrio, her town, city, or reservation. Nor, because of the play of differance, are any of these contexts static—they are interrelated and constantly shifting their relationships with one another.

But if all writing is collaborative and contextual in its composition, its reception is multiple, public, as well. This implies that classroom writing, like all writing, is, theoretically at least, available to anyone who can read. This theoretical availability can be realized in practice when students are encouraged to immerse their classroom writing into the flow of whatever public discourse is going on around them—in their institutions, workplaces, or communities. In fact, the dissemination of classroom writing into the discourse of the school or larger community may be one solution to the difficulty that haunts much student writing—its lack of motivation. A deconstructive pedagogy would engage students with issues that concern them directly, socially, and politically, and would direct the resulting discourses into the communities where such things matter: city or tribal council meetings, neighborhood groups, sorority meetings, school board meetings, landlords' associations, planning authorities, parents' groups, and the like.

Supplementation and Method

As my readers will have surmised by now, the deconstructive notion of supplementarity problematizes several canards that we use in our teaching. When we tell students to "say what they think" or to "write what they mean," we ignore the differing, supplemental facets of writing. More profoundly, differance and supplementarity problematize our easy separation of thought from language, content from form, meaning from expression, as well as the priority we assign to the first term in each opposition. However, deconstructive thought does not authorize a simple reversal of such priorities. To privilege form over content, for example, as much instruction based on current-traditional rhetoric does when it centers on "the paragraph" or "the thesis statement," is simply to be trapped within logocentrism once again.[5] More pertinently to our work as teachers, it is to misunderstand the nature of writing, which consists of signifiers, of signs representing signs representing signs, to infinity.

In *Dissemination*, Derrida has some provocative things to say about traditional notions about composing—called "method" by its seventeenth-century progenitors.[6] René Descartes, for example, proposed that composition could move in two directions. Analytic method—the method of inquiry—moved from effect to cause or from the specific to the general in such a way that an account of an analytic inquiry would exactly represent the way in which its results were discovered. Synthetic method—the method of presentation—moved from cause to effect or from general to specific; since conclusions had already been derived by means of analysis, the writer who worked with synthetic method could present them first. Throughout the methodical tradition, synthetic method was characterized as less valuable, and secondary to, analysis, since it was less original. Or, to use a favorite Derridean metaphor, the work of synthesis, gathering up and distributing what had previously been thought, was parasitic on, and reductive of, some more primary work. (Incidently, synthetic method was enshrined in traditional composition instruction as the five-paragraph essay, which moves from the general to the specific and which repeats for the reader some investigation that has always already taken place through other means.)

Derrida's comments on method come about in the context of his meditation on the puzzle of "the preface"—that part of the text which announces itself as coming before the text, "pre-speaking it," and yet which is ordinarily written after the text is finished. The preface claims to embody or summarize, or at least to introduce, what is contained in the rest of the work. This irruption of the preface into the composing process, and its dissemination into the "work itself," interests Derrida partly because it provides graphic testimony to the failure of composition ever to proceed in the orderly fashion dictated by method. The preface graphically signals that fact that "the text is no longer the snug airtight inside of an interiority or an identity-to-itself . . . but rather a different placement of the effects of opening and closing" (*Dis*, 36). Once again, texts move, open and close, come and go. They refuse to submit themselves to the stabilizing dichotomy of method, which would insist that texts are first thought, and that then they are written.

The traditional assumption that thinking precedes writing is derived directly from method, as this was delineated in the eighteenth-century rhetoric and logic texts that spawned traditional writing pedagogy. Recently, traditional composition textbooks have altered the language in which they couch their linear model of composing; the stage which nineteenth-century text writers called "thought" has been converted to "prewriting," and the older two-stage model ("thought" and "presentation") now has three stages: prewriting, writing, and rewriting. But this shift in nomenclature does not constitute a fundamental alteration in traditional notions about writing. "Prewriting techniques," or "heuristics," no matter how intricate, nevertheless presume that writers first engage in some activity that is not necessarily linguistic before they begin to write.

On a deconstructive model of the writing process, of course, beginnings, endings, middles and muddles are not quite so clearly demarcated. I wonder, for example, exactly when I began the "prewriting" for this book. Did it begin with my first reading of the *Grammatology* in 1978? Or with the composition of my first essay about deconstruction (in 1979)? And had I finished with prewriting when I entered the first lines of this essay into my computer? Not necessarily, since these lines came from a paper I had delivered at a meeting long before the composition of this essay was suggested to me. I was still rereading Derrida when I entered those hand-me-down lines, hoping they would break the spell of "his" voice over "mine." And, in contrast to the neat linear process dictated by method, I wrote what is now the second chapter first. Although that's not quite right because I found that I had to write parts of what is now the first chapter before I could finish the second. And so on.

And where does rewriting begin and end? As I write these words, the manuscript has already been reviewed and accepted for publication. That is, these words were not in the draft that its reviewers approved. They are here now because I've been asked to give more examples, in a revised version of the manuscript, of how deconstructive insights affect our thinking about writing pedagogy. And if the editors don't approve them when they do their rewriting of the manuscript, these words will be edited out and no other readers will ever read them. Certainly the reviewer who suggested such changes took part in the revision process. Other revisions will occur, of course, when readers rewrite the text after it is published, in reviews and, most likely, in letters addressed to me.

Genre Alert!

Traditional composition pedagogy is often organized along generic lines. Its textbooks devote chapters to the "expository essay," the "essay of comparison and contrast," the "persuasive essay," and the like. These and other conventional generic distinctions imply that certain formulaic constraints, embedded within a text, display the mode of thought or the kind of intention held by the writer. But the deconstructive critique of the nature of textuality disrupts a good deal of the traditional pedagogical thought that would channel the flow of the writing process into discreet generic categories, or would divide writing instruction itself into units, sections, or parts, "assignments," "themes," and "papers."

On the deconstructive account (and in process pedagogy as well) writing is conceived as continuous and dynamic. For pragmatic reasons, readers and writers entertain the illusion that the flow of writing is halted by its being stapled or paper-clipped and placed inside a plastic folder purchased from the bookstore. But this illusion of closure is only a convenient fiction. In keeping with its general suspicion of the imposition of limits on the movement of writing, then, the deconstructive critique of textuality also problematizes traditional use of generic categories.

Traditional composition teachers borrowed their list of generic categories from an eighteenth-century rhetorical theory that centralized the notion of authors' intentions. In this theory, genres such as "exposition" were thought to be discriminable from others such as "persuasion" or "expression" by means of the enshrinement within them of their authors' "aims." According to George Campbell, whose *Philosophy of Rhetoric* (1776) is an important progenitor of this tradition, such aims include enlightening the understanding, pleasing the imagination, moving the passions, or influencing the will. The text writers who borrowed Campbell's classification of "aims" soon began to associate each of them with a discriminate genre of discourse. That is, expository discourse appealed to the understanding, while narration and description appealed to the imagination, poetry inflamed the passions, and persuasive discourse influenced the will. Thus the metaphysical rhetorical theory that was spawned by Campbell's work supposed that the structure of a completed text could somehow graphically re-present its author's intention.

But, as we have seen, the notion of intention is a metaphysical fiction (this may be true of the notion of genre as well).[7] While generic distinctions are useful to readers, since they may (or may not) announce a text's lineage (the texts claimed as progenitors), they apparently do not entirely constrain the writing process as it occurs. When professional writers write, they ordinarily do not begin with generic constraints in mind. Often they do not know what sort of piece will result from their work; sometimes they are unsure even whether it will become prose or poetry.

And when an experienced writer is asked to write within a prescribed genre, such as a book review, she does not necessarily consult a conventional format that is prescribed for such pieces, although she may wish to do so in order to insure that her readers get all the kinds of commentary that they have learned to expect from such pieces of writing. During composition, however, she also considers her responses to the work in question, as well as the probable response of the audience for the review, and the context (journal or periodical) in which the review is to appear. If she is acquainted with the author, as often happens, she also considers that person's probable response to her review, and so on. She struggles to balance all of these constraints within the writing process, availing herself of whatever linguistic resources become apparent to her while she writes.

Thus, to insist that students begin the writing process within the conventions prescribed for them by mandated genres, such as exposition, is to simplify the nature of the writing process as professionals use it. It also denies the locatedness in place and time that characterizes rhetorical situations, insofar as students are encouraged to think of the generic classifications as more or less universally useful responses to any writing task. Further, it forecloses the possibility, at least within the scene of the classroom, that whatever the student is working on at the moment may turn itself into a poem, a letter home, a script, or an essay whose format does not appear in a textbook classification. To put this in deconstructive terms, genre-based pedagogy places restrictive boundaries on the movement of differance.

A deconstructive analytic also severely problematizes the status of some of the genres that are nearest and dearest to traditional pedagogy. For example, it compromises the traditional assumption that some writing (or all of it during early stages of composing) is "personal" or "expressive." Rather, all writing is done in order to be read eventually, even when it takes the form of notes or freewriting. The absence of an other, an audience, is precisely what motivates writing in the first place, even when that other is some imagined future version of one's "self," as in the case of notes jotted down for future reference. Too, this "future self" will be different from the "present self" because of its necessary immersion within the flow of differance.

If a deconstructive attitude problematizes the notion of the "personal essay," it poses nearly insuperable difficulties for the notion of "expository writing." Most of us who teach writing in American educational institutions work with courses or programs that utilize the term "expository writing." Exposition is a relatively new genre within the rhetorical tradition, having been invented in the late eighteenth century as an efficient generic means of conveying the results of scientific investigation to interested others. The "exposition" entailed in the term does not refer, of course, to writers' exposing their "thoughts," or "selves," as they are supposed to do in personal essays. No, it is some "subject" that is to be exposed (or, in a strange metaphoric opposition, "covered") by expository discourse. In the words of one of its early twentieth-century proponents, expository discourse amounts to a "succinct and orderly setting-forth of some piece of knowledge" (Baldwin 1902, 40). And according to the authors of a popular late-nineteenth-century textbook, a writer who undertakes the composition of expository discourse must "understand the subject under discussion better than his readers do." In exposition, "the writer's aim is to make others see the meaning of some idea as clearly as he himself sees it" (Scott and Denney 1909, 302).

Alexander Bain, who provided a powerful rationale for exposition during the middle of the nineteenth century, gave a more inclusive definition: for him, exposition was "the mode of handling applicable to knowledge or information in the form of what is called the Sciences," which, he was confident, were "each laid out on the plan of exhausting, in the most systematic array, all the information, respecting one department of nature" (1866, 147). Expository writing was to imitate this exhaustivity. Each expository essay was to lay before its readers, complete and entire, the writer's understanding of a given "subject."

If one accepts Derridean notions about writing, of course, "expository writing" is not thinkable. From a deconstructive point of view, writing does not "expose" much of anything, except perhaps itself. Nor can it "cover" (either in the sense of cloaking or exhausting) some subject that exists outside it. Derrida questions the ability of writing to represent anything outside itself, as well as the notion that some transcendental signifier can be found—mind, idea, soul, subject, knowledge, essence—which could authorize that representation. What precedes the act of writing is more writing; all that follows upon it is more writing (or reading). What writing does is extend itself, chain itself, into a series of signifiers whose proliferation can only be halted during the writing process by an act of will or sheer exhaustion.

Bain's project of systematizing and completing knowledge is the very one that Derrida sets out to attack. Derrida reads the necessity for logocentric cultures to think of knowledge as enclosed or encapsulated within essays or books as a grasp for totality, for closure, finally, for control; every writer wants to "have the last word." Again I quote Derrida (which in itself is sometimes an illuminating exercise in the inability of writing to expose anything):

> Good writing has therefore always been comprehended. . . . within a totality, and enveloped in a volume or a book. The idea of the book is the idea of a totality, finite or infinite, of the signifier; this totality of the signifier cannot be a totality, unless a totality constituted by the signified preexists it, supervises its inscriptions and its signs, and is independent of it in its ideality. (*OG*, 18)

In other words (Richard Rorty's), Derrida wants to demolish the notion of

> 'the book'—the notion of a piece of writing as aimed at accurate treatment of a subject, conveying a message which (in more fortunate circumstances) might have been conveyed by ostensive definition or by injecting knowledge straight into the brain. (1978, 146)

This goes equally well for the notions of "papers" and "themes," of course, which, on Derrida's model, cannot be construed as "containers" for some bit of "knowledge."

Expository writing, in its desire for transparency, completeness, and closure, participates in the Western metaphysical tradition in an almost ideal way; perhaps it is not too much of an exaggeration to say that exposition is the genre, par excellence, which secures the metaphysics of presence within the center of academic discourse. Vincent Leitch has remarked that the structure of any logocentric system "insures balance, coherence, and organization, all deployed around a controlled point," which is as nice a description of the five-hundred-word theme as will be found anywhere outside the textbook tradition (1983, 36). If Derrida's insights are worth entertaining, we writing teachers must consider an alternate possibility: to insist that our students compose balanced, coherent, and organized pieces of discourse is to hide a deception, a deception which radically misunderstands the nature of writing.

If traditional classes in "expository writing" play a bad joke on all of us, students are the most obvious butt of the joke. The tasks set for students in such a course are simply not possible to accomplish. First of all, assignments in exposition, if taken seriously, place students in the position of imitating writers who have devoted their careers to becoming expert in some field of inquiry. Such assignments, at the very least, trivialize the difficult process of acquiring scientific knowledge. But even more seriously, such assignments ask young people to learn to manage the terms and conventions of the discourse which surrounds a "subject" in a very short time and without assistance. Serious students try to work their way out of this dilemma by retreating to the library in order to read up on abortion, the war between Iraq and Iran, or whatnot. In Derridean terms, they try to enter into the chain of signification that surrounds, and amounts to, discourse about their subjects.

Students have another alternative, of course. They may attempt to fulfill an expository assignment by producing what Jasper Neel calls "anti-writing," where they "generate infinite numbers of texts that proclaim themselves as correct syntax, patterns of arrangement, and categories such as exposition" (1988, 149). Neel argues that students have learned that

> they can avoid writing altogether by providing shells with no interior: spelling, punctuation, sentences, paragraphs, structure, and coherence that are nothing but spelling, punctuation, sentences, paragraphs, structure and coherence. (165)

Faced by the enormity of trying to represent some "subject" in writing, then, some students adopt a strategy of display. As Neel observes, classes in expository writing "hardly ever generate any writing." Instead, students' texts simply announce that their authors are observing the syntactic and organizational rules they have been taught to follow. Anti-writing is a cynical version of the traditional Western attitude toward writing: it is the outside of an outside, writing thoroughly technologized, pure ritual.

Deconstructive Pedagogy as a Positive Science

The performance of this "reading" of traditional pedagogy may be as far as deconstruction will take us. I am not sure that a deconstructive pedagogy can be realized—the term is itself an oxymoron. Nevertheless, I can guess about some things a deconstructive pedagogy might be up to if it were thought of as a set of strategies for teaching.

First of all, it would reject the traditional model of authority that obtains in most American classrooms, where the teacher is both receptacle and translator of received knowledge.[8] At the very least, a deconstructive pedagogy would adopt the positions that knowledge is a highly contextualized activity which is constructed within groups, communities, or societies; that knowledge itself is a volatile construct, subject to alteration when contexts for knowing are altered; and that so-called "received" knowledge is just that—received. That is, the knowledge which is preferred and privileged at any given moment is so, simply because influential members of the concerned community have subscribed to it. A teacher who was convinced of the force of these assumptions would, no doubt, try to construct a classroom scene where they were daily allowed to come into play.

For another thing, a deconstructive pedagogy would reinforce the notion, as composition specialists would have it, that writing is a process. But it would interpret this slogan more profoundly to mean that the process that is writing is differentiation and not repetition of the same. The writing process differs to some extent with every situation or task; which also implies that no universally useful model or tactics for generating writing will ever be found. (At the very least, if such models exist, they exist in language, not minds, and are thus language-specific.) This does not mean that the writing process cannot be generalized about, of course. It simply means that writers must always take into account the constraints of the rhetorical situation in which they find themselves.

That writing is a process of differentiation also means that a syllabus for a writing class would always be in revision, would always be available for alteration as class members' writing changed the focus of the class. A syllabus for a semester- or year-long writing course that respects deconstructive attitudes toward writing would assume its relevance to all other writing being done, and formerly done, by teacher and students. No writing would be exempt from reading, rewriting, in such a class—papers for other classes, childhood poetry, the teacher's own work-in-progress. Nor would writing events that occur in connection with such classes be perceived as unrelated to one another. An "assignment" is writing by a teacher that calls for writing by students, which in turn calls for more writing by the teacher and so on and on. Freewritings, journals, essays, papers, are all part of a differentiating process that they only seem to halt by being put down on paper. They are all susceptible to revision, to incorporation into other texts, whether those other texts are written by the same or another or several writers at once. It may (should?) be that no "pieces" of writing are ever completed in such a class. The feeling that a writer can "finish" a piece of writing may simply disguise her exhaustion, her inability to go on, her lack of resources like time or money.

In other words, a deconstructive pedagogy would devise ways to engage students as active readers—that is, re-writers—of the teachers' writing—her course. It would encourage students to revise assignments and syllabi, to reject an assigned text and choose new ones. Such procedures would acknowledge the movement of differance, of writing, as it is worked out in the relation between the writers and readers of a text called "composition class." The changing relations that develop between teacher and students—and among students—as the writing class evolves, would mimic the changing relations that occur between words and sentences in a discourse as it is revised. Any readings that were undertaken in connection with such a class, literary or not, would also be seen as texts to be rewritten, to be incorporated into students' writing processes.

Further, a deconstructive pedagogy would treat the writing process exactly as it occurs always and everywhere: it would be as fully contextualized within the classroom as without. In composition class, English teachers are the ultimate audience for writing, much as are bosses, editors, and teachers of "content-area" classes. The traditional notion that composition prepares students for writing in the "real world" pretends that classroom writing is "practice" for some future "real writing." In other words, traditional assumptions always defer "real" writing, and this explains why so much student writing is unmotivated.

In a writing class governed by deconstructive attitudes, on the other hand, teachers would sensitize their students to the institutional realities in which they write, and they would treat the institutional situation as a "real-world" one where students are expected to learn a special brand of writing—academic discourse. And, since knowledge itself is always in flux, and since preferred knowledge is always inscribed by a culture in its institutions, students and teachers would examine the institutional ideology that governs their work: why "academic discourse" is preferred in school to whatever discourse(s) the students bring to school with them; why students might want to learn it (or not); why teachers are invested with institutional authority; why they are expected to give grades; how this constraint both interferes with, and encourages, the writing process.

In short, to adopt deconstructive attitudes toward writing and its teaching will not be an easy matter for either students or teachers, all of whom are accustomed to working within the constraints placed on them by institutions and a culture that subscribes to the metaphysics of presence. Perhaps the best to be hoped for is that a deconstructive critique demonstrates the necessity of continued interrogation of the strategies used to teach reading and writing. I can only hope that this essay has stimulated a few of its readers to engage in such a critique.

Appendix
How to Read Derrida

In her "Translator's Introduction" to *Dissemination*, Barbara Johnson identifies some of Derrida's rhetorical strategies in "Plato's Pharmacy" as follows: translation of a single word (wherein the Greek *pharmakon* is played with as both "poison" and "remedy"); anagrammatical texture (play with the etymology of a term); lateral association (which utilizes other contexts in which a given word is used across Plato's canon). Likewise, Derrida has also inscribed a set of themes of his own in this work: webs, textiles, textures, pens and surfaces, fathers and sons, sorcerers, magicians, and healers, and so on.

His realization that language is opaque, rather than transparent, explains why Derrida's works are so difficult. He uses incessant and extended punning, ellipsis, and self-reference to call attention to language, its cheats and maneuverings. He often speaks in tongues. Sometimes it is hard to tell whether one is reading Derrida, or whether he has put on Rousseau's—or Aristotle's, or Freud's—voice in order to speak through, around, and inside of that voice. In *Glas* (1974), his commentary on Hegel and Jean Genet is presented in two columns set side by side, so that they comment not only on their "subjects," but also on each other. They illustrate as well the illusion of "the book"—the illusion that books are stable containers of information whose margins and endpapers mark the last word, the end of all that can be said.

In short, it is best to approach Derrida's texts just as though they were literary texts. Readers should be alert to the appearance and reappearance of a favorite set of motifs, to Derrida's writing under the cover of some other writer's voice, to elliptical or unusual syntax, to coined terms or phrases, to play with the conventions of printing, and to bilingual punning.

I suggest that beginning readers of Derrida read together in groups of three or four. Read his work in short stretches, and then meet to discuss it. Since deconstruction is a strategy of reading, the real usefulness of reading together is established during the reading group's discussion, which is in itself a strategy of reading. Members of a group can also help each other to establish a glossary of Derridean terminology, voices, and motifs.

Perhaps I only think it best to begin with *Of Grammatology* since that is where my colleagues and I (Jay Farness, Jim Fitzmaurice, and Bryan Short) began to read Derrida. But the *Grammatology,* it still seems to me, offers Derrida's most sustained deconstruction of metaphysical notions about writing, and, as such, is central to the work of English teachers. Its translator's preface, written by Gayatri Spivak, is a succinct and lucid introduction to Derrida's work, and is very helpful to new readers who wish to locate Derrida within the philosophical tradition he is trying to deconstruct. (Don't be put off by the wealth of allusions in the introduction.)

But new readers might also start with the essays collected in *Writing and Difference,* especially those on Freud, Edmond Jabes, and Emmanuel Levinas. These essays are valuable less as commentary on individual writers than as early introductions to some of Derrida's pivotal notions: the composing process (which he calls "the scene of writing"), the question of the book, and the violence of the letter. This collection also contains his seminal deconstruction of structuralism: "Structure, Sign, and Play in the Discourse of the Human Sciences."

Really fervent readers might then want to move on to *Margins of Philosophy,* which reprints a number of essays of particular interest to English teachers, especially "Signature, Event, Context," which deconstructs the notion of written language as communication, and "White Mythology," a deconstruction of the Western notion of metaphor which centers on Aristotle's treatment of this figure in the *Rhetoric* and *Poetics.* I think that Derrida's most beautiful work, to date, is *Dissemination,* which includes an essay on Plato's *Phaedrus,* and an essay on the literary critical notion of mimesis. Barbara Johnson's translator's introduction to this work is very good, and helpful to newer readers of Derrida.

Readers who master these works should have an excellent understanding of Derrida and deconstruction. Those who wish to begin reading the texts which influenced Derrida's thought will find a handy collection in Mark C. Taylor's *Deconstruction in Context;* this work includes relevant readings from Kant, Hegel, Saussure, Nietzsche, Heidegger, Blanchot and others.

Notes

Chapter 1

1. Deconstruction thus validates the hermeneutic notion that archaic texts can never be read by modern readers exactly as they were interpreted by their first readers. For background on hermeneutic interpretation, see Hans-George Gadamer's *Truth and Method* (1985) and the final section of Richard Rorty's *Philosophy and the Mirror of Nature* (1979).

2. I am indebted to Janet Emig for this wonderful term.

3. In *A Preface to Literacy* (1987), Myron Tuman argues that some stretches of written language must appear within an immediate context in order to be meaningful at all. He gives the following example: "Meet me here at this time tomorrow with a stick this long" (15–16). I would argue, however, that even if this message were washed up on shore in a bottle, the finder would strive to construct a context for it that would inscribe it with some meaning—would imagine a sender, and an audience for it, in fact, as I immediately did when I read it, even situated as it was "inside" the covers of Tuman's book.

4. (*OG*, 81). A respected and accessible interpreter of the history of writing is Ignace Gelb, whose *A Study of Writing* (1952) was long the authoritative work on the subject in English. For more recent studies that take Derrida's insights into account, see Geoffrey Sampson, *Writing Systems* (1985) and Roy Harris, *The Origin of Writing* (1986). For a study of how ancient scripts are deciphered, see Maurice Pope, *The Story of Archeological Decipherment* (1975). See also Derrida on Condillac (*Archeology of the Frivolous*) and Warburton ("Scribble").

Chapter 2

1. "Post-structuralism" was once a term that applied to any systematic critique of a methodology called "structuralism." During the mid-twentieth century, structuralist thought was prominent in linguistics, anthropology, psychology, philosophy, and literary criticism. Structuralists assume that (presumably universal) laws, or structures of laws, govern human activity and that these laws can be ferreted out by determined investigation of human systems such as language or kinship. Given Derrida's critiques of the work of two premiere structuralists, Ferdinand de Saussure and Claude Lévi-Strauss, deconstruction is, if not preeminent among post-structuralisms, certainly a forceful division of poststructural thought. The term "post-structuralism" subsequently evolved into a designation that could be used for any theory or methodology which offered a critique of modernist notions such as the sovereign self. In this guise "post-structuralism" is equivalent to "post-

modernism." See Michael Lane's "Introduction" in his *Introduction to Structuralism* (1970) for a lucid description of structuralism; another good collection of structuralist texts can be found in DeGeorge and DeGeorge, *The Structuralists: From Marx to Lévi-Strauss* (1972). For an account of the relation of structuralism to literary criticism and its development into post-structuralism, see John Sturrock, ed., *Structuralism and Since: Lévi-Strauss to Derrida* (1979).

2. (1982, 37). In *Marxism and Deconstruction*, Ryan demonstrates conclusively that Derridean deconstruction has a political agenda. That it also has ramifications for pedagogy has been demonstrated in a number of works. Among those not mentioned elsewhere in this essay are G. Douglas Atkins's and Michael Johnson's *Writing and Reading Differently: Deconstruction and the Teaching of Composition and Literature* (1985) and Barbara Johnson's *The Pedagogical Imperative* (1981).

3. Those who undertake to criticize deconstruction often don't take the time to read Derrida's (admittedly difficult) texts, relying instead for their assessment of deconstruction on the literary criticism produced by the Yale critics, or on books about Derrida. And those who do, and who recognize the threat that deconstruction poses to institutionalized literary criticism and traditional definitions of English studies, often choose to misunderstand its implications. For example, in *Does Deconstruction Make Any Difference?* (1987), Michael Fischer argues that Derrida has no right to complain about misreadings of his texts, since a deconstructive viewpoint mandates the equivocality of all texts (40ff). That texts are susceptible to multiple interpretations does not entail that all readings are good readings, or that texts cannot be read at all.

4. I am aware that my casual use of the terms "theory" and "practice" overlooks the controversy over the relevance of theory to anything at all. To call new criticism a "theory of textuality" is to make no more claims for it than to say that it offers a coherent description of how an ideal text ought to look. For a polemic examination of the problem of the status of theory, see W. J. T. Mitchell, ed., *Against Theory: Literary Studies and the New Pragmatism* (1985), especially the contribution by Stanley Fish entitled "Consequences."

5. The theory of textuality advanced by current-traditional rhetoric has all sorts of ideological implications that we are only now beginning to understand. At the very least, it reinforces the logocentric authority ascribed to science. For an introduction to current-traditional rhetoric and its ideological implications, see James A. Berlin, *Writing Instruction in Nineteenth-Century American Colleges* (1984). For examinations of the ideological implications of process pedagogy, see Greg Myers, "Reality, Consensus, and Reform in the Rhetoric of Composition Teaching" (1986) and Myron C. Tuman, "Class, Codes, and Composition: Basil Bernstein and the Critique of Pedagogy" (1988).

Chapter 3

1. I am engaging in nothing so ambitious here as a critique of traditional pedagogy, when "critique" is defined as it is by Barbara Johnson: "A critique of any theoretical system . . . is an analysis that focuses on the grounds of that system's possibility. The critique reads backwards from what seems natural, obvious, self-evident, or universal, in order to show that these things have their history, their reasons for being the way they are, their effects on

what follows from them, and that the starting point is not a natural given but a cultural construct, usually blind to itself (*Dis*, xv). It may well be the case that I shift away from deconstructive analysis in the latter portion of this essay, toward a hermeneutic interpretation of writing pedagogy.

2. For historical examinations of the authority invested in authorship during the modern era, see Timothy Reiss, *The Discourse of Modernism* (1982), and Michel Foucault, "What is an Author?" (1979). For a readable explication of post-modern critiques of the sovereign self, written by a philosopher, see Vincent Descombes, *Modern French Philosophy* (1980).

3. Spivak explicitly connects masculine and feminine roles with those of writer and reader, respectively. Indeed the phallic overtones of the very act of writing, which begins with pen (instrument, tool) inscribing paper (space, potentially fertile ground), are obvious enough. Derrida has also exploited the sexual imagery associated with the writing process. See "The Question of Style" (1977). Nor has the appropriateness of sexual imagery for the rhetorical process escaped rhetoricians: see Wayne Brockriede's "Arguers as Lovers" (1972).

4. See Lee Odell and Dixie Goswami, *Writing in Non-Academic Settings* (1985), especially Paul V. Anderson, "What Survey Research Tells Us about Writing at Work" (50–51).

5. The "ideal text" posited by traditional composition pedagogy constitutes an interesting elevation of form over content, thus reversing the traditional metaphysical hierarchy. I suspect that this came about for institutional as well as political reasons. Teachers of composition have always been overworked; if they could reduce their commentary on student papers to formulaic considerations, ignoring "content," they expedited the work of grading papers. The notion that teachers ought to be neutral in their response to students' arguments also protects teachers (and the institutions they represent) from having to take positions within the social or political discourse which is carried on in the culture surrounding the academy.

6. (*Dis*, 36–37). In good disseminatory fashion, I am paraphrasing Derrida, who, in a footnote to "Outwork," is quoting a "reply" made by Descartes to his critics.

7. For an examination of the problem of genre, see Derrida's "The Law of Genre," as well as the rest of the essays collected in *Glyph 7* (1980).

8. For explications of the historical and political reasoning that makes this move necessary, see Gregory Ulmer, *Applied Grammatology* (1985, 157–72); and Ryan, *Marxism and Deconstruction*, chapter 7, "Reason and Counterrevolution." I realize that many of the suggestions I make here are subversive of institutionalized writing instruction. Since schools are a mainstay of logocentrism, the adoption of deconstructive attitudes toward institutional pedagogies is necessarily a subversive act. For a brilliant critique of the thoroughness with which educational institutions and their students have absorbed the metaphysics of presence, see Jasper Neel, *Plato, Derrida, Writing* (1988).

Glossary

To define terms is to commit a metaphysical act, since definitions assume that limits can be drawn around meanings. However, the editors at NCTE insisted that definitions of a few key terms would make this text more accessible to its readers. I bow to their wishes and provide this brief glossary. Readers are forewarned, however, that the definitions listed here are simplifications of enormously complex terms that cannot be easily understood outside of the historical context in which Derrida and others employ them.

Arche-writing: Derrida's term for human consciousness or being. The terms "consciousness" and "being" are integral to the metaphysics of presence. Derrida uses the term "writing" to underscore the fact that consciousness itself is made possible by the signing function of language. Arche-writing is sometimes a synonym (if such things exist) for "differance."

Differance: A pun in French, combining the meanings of the English terms "difference" and "deferring." Differance then alludes to (1) the tendency of meaning to inhere in items which differ from one another, and (2) the tendency of language to always put off, or preclude, the discovery of any final or authoritative interpretation of itself. In a larger sense, differance characterizes the movement of human consciousness and knowledge.

Erasure: Derrida employs the French phrase *"sous rature"* (under erasure) when he wishes to interrogate the ordinary or casual use of crucial cultural terms, such as "self" or "being." He sometimes indicates that a term has been placed under erasure by writing a large "X" across its face. Thus the term is still present (we can still see it on the page), but its ordinary uses have been put into question, or "erased" at the same time. This little graphic project is only one means by which Derrida indicates the difficulty inherent in any radical re-thinking of the metaphysics of presence, or in erasing the cultural effects of any of its crucial terms; it also reminds readers of the "absence" or "trace" that resides at the origin of human writing.

Inscription: Literally, writing on a page; imposing one's mark upon a surface. More generally, inscription refers to human impact on an environment—inscription occurs by means of dance, sex, speech, photography, architecture, politics—any human sphere that can be demarcated or delineated.

Metaphysics of Presence: The set of assumptions about mind, language, and being which has characterized Western philosophy since Plato (see chapter 1).

Occulting: "Hiding" or "forgetting" a term and its uses. Usually terms that are occulted are part of a binary dichotomy. The preference for the privileged term in the pairing blots out cultural awareness of its (nevertheless necessary) partner. Within the metaphysics of presence, the second term in each of the following pairs has occasionally or always been "occulted": male/female, speaking/writing, thought/language.

Supplementation: "Substitution" is not a synonym for supplementation, since the latter term also signifies a dual process of filling up a space which was not completely occupied, as well as expanding that space to make room for new supplements. Supplementation thus names one movement of differance. The notions of supplementation and differance, in fact, problematize the assumption that synonyms—names which exactly substitute for other names—can be found in language at all. Roget's *Thesaurus* provides a splendid example of the supplementary movement of language, insofar as its lists of supposedly similar terms actually demonstrate how words differ from one another, proliferating new shades of meaning in the process.

Bibliography

In citing works in the text, notes, and bibliography, short titles have been used to refer to frequently cited works by Derrida. These works are identified by the following abbreviations:

Dis	*Dissemination* (1981)
MP	*The Margins of Philosophy* (1982)
OG	*Of Grammatology* (1976)
WD	*Writing and Difference* (1975)

List of Works Cited

Abrams, M. H. "The Limits of Pluralism: Deconstructive Angel." *Critical Inquiry* 3 (1977): 425–38.

Atkins, G. Douglas and Michael Johnson, eds. *Writing and Reading Differently: Deconstruction and the Teaching of Composition and Literature.* Lawrence: University Press of Kansas, 1985.

Bain, Alexander. *English Composition and Rhetoric.* London: Longmans, 1866.

Baldwin, Charles S. *A College Manual of Rhetoric.* New York: Longmans, 1902.

Berlin, James A. *Writing Instruction in Nineteenth-Century American Colleges.* Carbondale: Southern Illinois University Press, 1984.

Brockriede, Wayne. "Arguers as Lovers." *Colorado Journal of Educational Research* 2 (1972): 3–7.

Cain, William E. *The Crisis in Criticism: Theory, Literature, and Reform in English Studies.* Baltimore: Johns Hopkins University Press, 1984.

Campbell, George. *The Philosophy of Rhetoric.* Edited by Lloyd F. Bitzer. Carbondale: Southern Illinois University Press, 1963.

Covino, William. "Making Differences in the Composition Class: A Philosophy of Invention." *Freshman English News* 10 (1981): 1–13.

Culler, Jonathan. *On Deconstruction: Theory and Criticism after Structuralism.* Ithaca: Cornell University Press, 1982.

de Man, Paul. *Allegories of Reading: Figural Language in Rousseau, Nietzsche, Rilke, and Proust.* New Haven: Yale University Press, 1979.

DeGeorge, Richard T. and Fernande M. DeGeorge, eds. *The Structuralists: From Marx to Lévi-Strauss.* Garden City, New York: Anchor, 1972.

Derrida, Jacques. *Archeology of the Frivolous: Reading Condillac.* Pittsburgh: Duquesne University Press, 1980.

———. *Dissemination.* Translated by Barbara Johnson. Chicago: University of Chicago Press, 1981.

———. *Glas.* Translated by John P. Leavey, Jr. and Richard Rand. Lincoln: University of Nebraska Press, 1986.

———. "La Loi du genre/The Law of Genre." In *Glyph 7*, 176–229. Baltimore: Johns Hopkins University Press, 1980.

———. *The Margins of Philosophy.* Translated by Alan Bass. Chicago: University of Chicago Press, 1982.

———. *Of Grammatology.* Translated by Gayatri Chakravorty Spivak. Baltimore: Johns Hopkins University Press, 1976.

———. *Positions.* Translated by Alan Bass. Chicago: University of Chicago Press, 1981.

———. "The Question of Style." In *The New Nietzsche: Contemporary Styles of Interpretation*, edited by David Allison, 176–89. New York: Delta, 1977.

———. "Scribble (writing-power)." Translated by Cary Plotkin. *Yale French Studies* 58 (1979): 116–47.

———. "Signature, Event, Context." In *Glyph 1*, 172–97. Baltimore: Johns Hopkins University Press, 1977. (Reprinted in *The Margins of Philosophy.*)

———. "The Time of a Thesis: Punctuations." In *Philosophy in France Today*, edited by Alan Montefiore, 34–50. Cambridge, England: Cambridge University Press, 1983.

———. "The White Mythology: Metaphor in the Text of Philosophy. *New Literary History* 6 (1974): 7–74. (Reprinted in *Margins.*)

———. *Writing and Difference.* Translated by Alan Bass. Chicago: University of Chicago Press, 1975.

Descombes, Vincent. *Modern French Philosophy.* Translated by L. Scott-Fox and J. M. Harding. Cambridge, England: Cambridge University Press, 1980.

Eagleton, Terry. *Walter Benjamin: Or Towards a Revolutionary Criticism.* London: Verso, 1981.

Fischer, Michael. *Does Deconstruction Make Any Difference?* Bloomington: Indiana University Press, 1987.

Foucault, Michel. "What is an Author?" In *Textual Strategies: Perspectives in Post-Structural Criticism*, edited by Josue V. Harari, 141–60. London: Methuen and Company, 1979.

Gadamer, Hans-Georg. *Truth and Method.* New York: Crossroad Publishing Company, 1985.

Gelb, Ignace J. *A Study of Writing.* Rev. ed. Chicago: University of Chicago Press, 1952.

Harned, Jon. "Post-structuralism and the Teaching of Composition." *Freshman English News* 15 (1986): 10–16.

Harris, Roy. *The Origin of Writing.* London: Duckworth, 1986.

Johnson, Barbara, ed. *The Pedagogical Imperative. Yale French Studies* (63), 1981.

Knoblauch, C. H. and Lil Brannon. *Rhetorical Traditions and the Teaching of Writing.* Montclair, N.J.: Boynton-Cook Publishers, 1984.

Krieger, Murray. "The Recent Revolution in Theory and the Survival of the Literary Discourses." In *The State of the Discipline, 1970's–1980's*, edited by Jasper Neel, 27–34. (Special Issue of the *ADE Bulletin* 62 (1979): 27–34.)

Lane, Michael, ed. *Introduction to Structuralism.* New York: Basic Books, 1970.

Leitch, Vincent. "Deconstruction and Pedagogy." In Atkins and Johnson, 16–26.

———. *Deconstructive Criticism: An Advanced Introduction.* New York: Columbia University Press, 1983.

McCormick, Kathleen, Gary Waller, and Linda Flower. *Reading Texts: Reading, Responding, Writing.* Lexington, Mass.: D. C. Heath, 1987.

Mitchell, W. J. T., ed. *Against Theory: Literary Studies and the New Pragmatism.* Chicago: University of Chicago Press, 1985.

Miller, J. Hillis. "The Critic as Host." *Critical Inquiry* 3 (1977): 439–47. Revised and reprinted in *Deconstruction and Criticism,* edited by Geoffrey Hartman, 217–53.

———. "Composition and Decomposition: Deconstruction and the Teaching of Writing." In *Composition and Literature: Bridging the Gap,* edited by Winifred Bryan Horner, 38–56. Chicago: University of Chicago Press, 1983.

Miller, Susan. "Is There a Text in This Class?" *Freshman English News* 11 (1982): 20–23.

Myers, Greg. "Reality, Consensus, and Reform in the Rhetoric of Composition Teaching." *College English* 48 (1986): 154–74.

Neel, Jasper. *Plato, Derrida, Writing.* Carbondale: Southern Illinois University Press, 1988.

Norris, Christopher. *Deconstruction: Theory and Practice.* London: Methuen, 1982.

North, Stephen. *The Making of Knowledge in Composition.* Montclair, N.J.: Boynton-Cook, 1987.

Odell, Lee and Dixie Goswami, eds. *Writing in Non-Academic Settings.* New York: The Guilford Press, 1985.

Plato. "The Phaedrus." In *The Collected Dialogues of Plato,* edited by Edith Hamilton and Hamilton Cairns, 475–525. Princeton, N.J.: Princeton University Press, 1963.

Pope, Maurice. *The Story of Archeological Decipherment: From Egyptian Hieroglyphs to Linear B.* New York: Charles Scribners' Sons, 1975.

Reiss, Timothy. *The Discourse of Modernism.* Ithaca: Cornell University Press, 1982.

Rorty, Richard. *Philosophy and the Mirror of Nature.* Princeton, N.J.: Princeton University Press, 1979.

———. "Philosophy as a Kind of Writing." *New Literary History* 10 (1978): 141–61.

Ryan, Michael. *Marxism and Deconstruction: A Critical Articulation.* Baltimore: Johns Hopkins University Press, 1982.

Sampson, Geoffrey. *Writing Systems: A Linguistic Introduction.* London: Hutchinson, 1985.

Scholes, Robert. "Deconstruction and Criticism." *Critical Inquiry* 14 (1988): 278–95.

Scholes, Robert, Nancy Comley, and Gregory Ulmer. *Text Book.* New York: St. Martin's Press, 1988.

Scott, Fred Newton and Joseph Villiers Denney. *Paragraph-Writing: A Rhetoric for Colleges.* New ed. Boston: Allyn and Bacon, [1893] 1909.

Spivak, Gayatri Chakravorty. "Revolutions That As Yet Have No Model: Derrida's 'Limited Inc.' " *Diacritics* 10 (1980): 29–49.

———. "Love Me, Love My Ombre, Elle." *Diacritics* 14 (1984): 19–36.

Sturrock, John C., ed. *Structuralism and Since: Lévi-Strauss to Derrida.* Oxford: Oxford University Press, 1979.

Taylor, Mark C., ed. *Deconstruction in Context: Literature and Philosophy.* Chicago: University of Chicago Press, 1986.

Tuman, Myron C. "Class, Codes, and Composition: Basil Bernstein and the Critique of Pedagogy." *College Composition and Communication* 39 (1988): 42–51.

———. *A Preface to Literacy: An Enquiry into Pedagogy, Practice, and Progress.* University, Alabama: Alabama University Press, 1987.

Ulmer, Gregory. *Applied Grammatology: Post(e)-Pedagogy from Jacques Derrida to Joseph Beuys.* Baltimore: Johns Hopkins University Press, 1985.

Warnock, Tilly. "How I Write." In *Writers on Writing,* edited by Tom Waldrep, 305–15. New York: Random House, 1985.

White, Edward M. "Post-Structural Literary Criticism and the Response to Student Writing." *College Composition and Communication* 35 (1984): 186–195.

Winterowd, W. Ross. "Post-structuralism and Composition," *Pre/Text* 4 (1983): 85–95.

———. "The Purification of Literature and Rhetoric." *College English* 49 (1987): 257–73.

Some Works by Derrida Not Cited in the Text

"The Conflict of Faculties." In *Languages of Knowledge and Languages of Knowledge and of Inquiry,* edited by Michael Riffaterre. New York: Columbia University Press, 1982. (On Kant and authority.)

The Ear of the Other: Otobiography, Transference, Translation. Edited by Christie V. McDonald and translated by Peggy Kamuf. New York: Schocken Books, 1985. (Interviews and discussions.)

"Economimesis." *Diacritics* 11 (1981): 3–25. (On Kant.)

Edmund Husserl's Origin of Geometry. Translated by Edward Leavey. Stony-brook: Hays, 1978.

"Limited Inc. abc." In *Glyph* 2, 162–254. Baltimore: Johns Hopkins University Press, 1978. (A reply to John Searle, who had attacked Derrida's reading of J. L. Austin in "Signature, Event, Context.")

"Living On—Border Lines." In *Deconstruction and Criticism,* edited by Geoffrey Hartman, 75–176. New York: The Seabury Press, 1979. (On Shelley— ostensibly.)

The Post Card: From Socrates to Freud and Beyond. Translated by Alan Bass. Chicago: University of Chicago Press, 1987.

"L'Age de Hegel." In *Qui a Peur de la Philosophie?,* 73–107. Paris: Flammarion, 1977. (Writing with members of GREPH [Groupe de Recherches sur l'Enseignement Philosophique].) (On teaching.)

Speech and Phenomena and Other Essays on Husserl's Theory of Signs. Translated by David Allison. Evanston: Northwestern University Press, 1973.

Spurs: Nietzsche's Styles. Translated by Barbara Harlow. Chicago: University of Chicago Press, 1979.

The Truth in Painting. Translated by Geoff Bennington and Ian McLeod. Chicago: University of Chicago Press, 1987.

On Derrida and Deconstruction

Arac, Jonathan, and others. *The Yale Critics: Deconstruction in America*. Minneapolis: University of Minnesota Press, 1983.

Atkins, G. Douglas. *Reading Deconstruction: Deconstructive Reading*. Lexington: University of Kentucky Press, 1983.

Butler, Christopher. *Interpretation, Deconstruction, and Ideology: An Introduction to Some Current Issues in Literary Theory*. Oxford: Clarendon Press, 1984.

Cain, William E. "Deconstruction in America: The Recent Literary Criticism of J. Hillis Miller." *College English* 41 (1979): 367–82.

Cascardi, A. J. "Skepticism and Deconstruction." *Philosophy and Literature* 8 (1984): 1–14.

Crowley, Sharon. "Of Gorgias and Grammatology." *College Composition and Communication* 30 (1979): 279–84.

———. "Post-structuralism and Composition." *Pre/Text* 5 (1984): 185–95.

———. "writing and Writing." In Atkins and Johnson, 93–100.

de Man, Paul. *Blindness and Insight: Essays in the Rhetoric of Contemporary Criticism*. New York: Oxford University Press, 1971.

Eagleton, Terry. *Literary Theory: An Introduction*. Minneapolis: University of Minnesota Press, 1983.

Felperin, Howard. *Beyond Deconstruction: The Uses and Abuses of Literary Theory*. Oxford: Clarendon Press, 1985.

Ferguson, Frances. "Reading Heidegger: Jacques Derrida and Paul de Man." *Boundary* 2 (1976): 593–610.

Foley, Barbara. "The Politics of Deconstruction." In *Rhetoric and Form: Deconstruction at Yale*, edited by Robert Con Davis and Ronald Schliefer, 113–34. Norman: University of Oklahoma Press, 1985.

Fynsk, Christopher. "A Decelebration of Philosophy." *Diacritics* 8 (1978): 80–90.

Gasche, Rodolphe. "Deconstruction as Criticism." In *Glyph* 6, 177–216. Baltimore: Johns Hopkins University Press, 1979.

Goodheart, Eugene. *The Skeptic Disposition in Contemporary Criticism*. Princeton, N.J.: Princeton University Press, 1985.

Hartman, Geoffrey. "How Creative Should Literary Criticism Be?" *New York Times Book Review* (5 April 1981): 11, 24–5.

———. *Saving the Text: Literature/Philosophy/Derrida*. Baltimore: Johns Hopkins University Press, 1981.

Harvey, Irene. *Derrida and the Economy of Différance*. Bloomington: Indiana University Press, 1986..

Johnson, Barbara. *The Critical Difference: Essays in the Contemporary Rhetoric of Reading.* Baltimore: Johns Hopkins University Press, 1980.

Kaufer, David and Gary Waller. "To Write Is to Read Is to Write, Right?" In Atkins and Johnson, 66–92.

Krupnick, Mark. *Displacement: Derrida and After.* Bloomington: Indiana University Press, 1983.

Leitch, Vincent B. "The Lateral Dance: The Deconstructive Criticism of J. Hillis Miller." *Critical Inquiry* 6 (1980): 593–607.

Lentricchia, Frank. *After the New Criticism.* Chicago: University of Chicago Press, 1980.

Lewis, Philip. "The Post-structuralist Condition." *Diacritics* 12 (1982): 1–24.

McDonald, Christie. "Jacques Derrida's Reading of Rousseau." *The Eighteenth Century* 20 (1970): 82–95.

Miller, J. Hillis. "Ariadne's Broken Woof." *Georgia Review* 31 (1977): 44–60.

———. "Ariadne's Thread: Repetition and the Narrative Line." *Critical Inquiry* 3 (1976): 57–78.

———. "The Search for Grounds in Literary Study." *Genre* 17 (1984): 19–36.

———. "Stevens' Rock and Criticism as Cure." *Georgia Review* 30 (1976): 5–33.

Norris, Christopher. *The Contest of Faculties: Philosophy and Theory after Deconstruction.* New York: Methuen, 1985.

Rand, Richard. "Geraldine." In *Glyph 3*, 74–97. Baltimore: Johns Hopkins University Press, 1978.

Ray, William. *Literary Meaning: From Phenomenology to Deconstruction.* Oxford: Blackwell, 1984.

Rorty, Richard. "Deconstruction and Circumvention." *Critical Inquiry* 11 (1984): 1–23.

Searle, John. "Reiterating the Differences: A Reply to Derrida." In *Glyph 1*, 198–208. Baltimore: Johns Hopkins University Press, 1977.

Scholes, Robert. *Textual Power: Literary Theory and the Teaching of English.* New Haven: Yale University Press, 1985.

Spivak, Gayatri. "Reading the World: Literary Studies in the 1980's." *College English* 43 (1981): 671–79.

Young, Robert, ed. *Untying the Text: A Post-Structuralist Reader.* London: Routledge and Kegan Paul, 1981.

Some Exemplary Deconstructive Readings

Atkins, G. Douglas. *Quests of Difference: Reading Pope's Poems.* Lexington: University Press of Kentucky, 1986.

Chase, Cynthia. "The Decomposition of the Elephants: Double-Reading *Daniel Deronda*." *PMLA* 93 (1978): 215–27.

Flores, Anthony. *The Rhetoric of Doubtful Authority: Deconstructive Readings of Self-Questioning Narratives, St. Augustine to Faulkner.* Ithaca: Cornell University Press, 1984.

Jacobs, Carol. "The (Too) Good Soldier: 'A Real Story.'" In *Glyph 3*, 32–51. Baltimore: Johns Hopkins University Press, 1978.

Miller, J. Hillis. *Fiction and Repetition: Seven English Novels*. Cambridge: Harvard University Press, 1982.

Ryan, Michael. "The Question of Autobiography in Cardinal Newman's *Apologia pro vita sua*." *Georgia Review* 31 (1977): 672–99.

Spivak, Gayatri. "Sex and History in *The Prelude* (1805): Books Nine to Thirteen." *Texas Studies in Language and Literature* 23 (1981): 324–60.

Sussman, Henry. *Franz Kafka: Geometrician of Metaphor*. Madison: Coda Press, 1979.

———. "The Deconstructionist as Politician: Melville's *The Confidence Man*." In *Glyph 4*, 32–56. Baltimore: Johns Hopkins University Press, 1978.

Author

Sharon Crowley is professor of English at Northern Arizona University. She has taught high school English and has served as editor of the *Arizona English Bulletin* and director of NCTE's Commission on Composition. Professor Crowley has published widely on rhetoric and composition theory and the history of rhetoric and composition studies.